はしがき

　本書は第一学習社発行の英語教科書「CREATIVE English Communication II」に完全準拠したワークブックです。各パート1ページで，授業傍用と授業後の復習として役立つ練習問題のみならず，各レッスンの最後には総合問題も用意しました。また教科書本文のディクテーションも設けました。

CONTENTS

Part 1 教科書 p.6〜p.7 　/54

A Write the English words to match the Japanese. 【知識・技能（語彙）】（各 2 点）

1. .... 形 持続可能な
2. .... 名 開発 B1
3. .... 形 女性の A2
4. .... 動 …に出席する B1
5. .... 名 影響 A2
6. .... 動 …を代表する A2

B Choose the word whose underlined part's sound is different from the other three.

【知識・技能（発音）】（各 2 点）

1. ア. f<u>e</u>male 　イ. l<u>ea</u>der 　ウ. repr<u>e</u>sent 　エ. uncl<u>ea</u>n
2. ア. c<u>ou</u>ntry 　イ. en<u>ou</u>gh 　ウ. y<u>ou</u>ng 　エ. y<u>ou</u>th
3. ア. <u>h</u>igh 　イ. <u>h</u>ometown 　ウ. <u>h</u>onor 　エ. <u>h</u>orror

C Complete the following English sentences to match the Japanese.

【知識・技能（表現・文法）】（完答・各 3 点）

1. 私たちのクラブを代表するのに私はケンを選びたい。

   I'd like to (　　　　) Ken (　　　　) represent our club.
2. ボランティア活動はあなたの人生に大きな意味をもたらすでしょう。

   Volunteer work will (　　　　) (　　　　) big (　　　　) to your life.
3. 彼がその問題の責任を取るべきだと思います。

   I think he should (　　　　) (　　　　) for the matter.

D Arrange the words in the proper order to match the Japanese.

【知識・技能（表現・文法）】（各 4 点）

1. スーは私の親友のひとりです。

   Sue is (close / friends / my / of / one).

   ----
2. 彼にロンドンまでの旅費を支援してもらったらどうですか。

   Why don't you (have / him / support / to / trip / your) London?

   ----
3. 最善の解決策は，持続可能な社会に向けて新しい科学技術を使うことだと思います。

   I believe the best solution (for / is / new / technology / to / use) a sustainable
   society.

E Fill in each blank with a suitable word from the passage. 【思考力・判断力・表現力（内容）】（各 5 点）

1. Eva Jones (　　　　) the United Nations Youth Climate Summit.
2. She was inspired to be an (　　　　) for the earth and the living things on it.
3. She thinks we have the power to stop the bad (　　　　) that are changing the
   earth's climate.

Part 2 教科書 p.8

/54

A Write the English words to match the Japanese. 【知識・技能（語彙）】（各2点）

1. .... 副 ますます B1
2. .... 名 本部 B2
3. .... 動 申し込む A2
4. .... 動 …を評価する B2
5. .... 名 乗り物 B1
6. .... 名 参加者 B1

B Choose the word whose underlined part's sound is different from the other three.

【知識・技能（発音）】（各2点）

1. ア．d<u>ea</u>l　　イ．h<u>ea</u>dquarters　　ウ．incr<u>ea</u>singly　　エ．l<u>ea</u>der
2. ア．l<u>o</u>cate　　イ．<u>o</u>nly　　ウ．<u>o</u>ver　　エ．territ<u>o</u>ry
3. ア．carbon-neutral　　イ．cl<u>i</u>mate　　ウ．part<u>i</u>cipant　　エ．veh<u>i</u>cle

C Complete the following English sentences to match the Japanese.

【知識・技能（表現・文法）】（完答・各3点）

1. その都市は交通渋滞の問題に対処しなければならない。

   The city has to (　　　　) (　　　　) the problem of traffic jams.

2. この情報に基づくと，結論に達することが可能だ。

   It is possible to reach a conclusion (　　　　) the (　　　　) (　　　　) this information.

3. だれも傘をさしていません。言い換えると，雨がやんだということです。

   No one is using an umbrella. (　　　　) (　　　　) (　　　　), it stopped raining.

D Arrange the words in the proper order to match the Japanese.

【知識・技能（表現・文法）】（各4点）

1. 食事の後においしいケーキが出たので，私は幸運に感じた。

   I felt lucky because (a / by / cake / delicious / followed / the meal / was).

   ....

2. その問題に対して私たちはどう責任を持つべきか助言をいただけますか。

   Will you give us some advice on (how / responsibility / should / take / we) for the matter?

   ....

3. その企業は，騒音がほとんど出ない車を開発することに成功した。

   The company succeeded in developing (cars / emit / little / noise / which).

   ....

E Fill in each blank with a suitable word from the passage.

【思考力・判断力・表現力（内容）】（各5点）

1. The United Nations Youth Climate Summit was (　　　　) at the UN Headquarters.
2. Over 7,000 young people (　　　　) to the Youth Climate Summit.
3. The "Green Ticket" winners used transportation which was as (　　　　) as possible.

Part 3   教科書 p.10

/54

A Write the English words to match the Japanese. 【知識・技能（語彙）】（各 2 点）

1. .... 動 …を分類する B2
2. .... 動 …を説得する B1
3. .... 名 代用品 B1
4. .... 動 …を断る B1
5. .... 名 出席者
6. .... 動 …を防ぐ A2

B Choose the word whose stressed syllable is different from the other three.

【知識・技能（発音）】（各 2 点）

1. ア．fel-low   イ．per-suade   ウ．pre-vent   エ．re-fuse
2. ア．at-tend-ee   イ．em-pow-er   ウ．pol-lu-tion   エ．re-cy-cle
3. ア．al-ter-na-tive イ．par-tic-i-pant   ウ．phi-los-o-phy   エ．ter-ri-to-ry

C Complete the following English sentences to match the Japanese.

【知識・技能（表現・文法）】（完答・各 3 点）

1. 私は 5 歳のときにピアノの練習を始めた。

   I started practicing the piano (   ) the (   ) of five.

2. 教授は私たちの前でスピーチをして，環境に配慮した生活様式についての考えを勧めた。

   The professor made a speech in front of us, (   ) his idea of an eco-friendly lifestyle.

3. 私たちは，優れたチームワークを作ることを目指して取り組める人を探しています。

   We are looking for someone who can (   ) (   ) building excellent teamwork.

D Arrange the words in the proper order to match the Japanese.

【知識・技能（表現・文法）】（各 4 点）

1. あわてなくてもよいように，早く起きるべきですよ。

   You should (don't / early / get up / have / so / that / to / you) hurry.

   ----

2. 今週末は海ではなく山に行きませんか。

   Why don't we (a mountain / go / instead / of / the sea / to) this weekend?

   ----

3. 健はその問題の解決に，彼らに別の手法をとるように説得しようとしている。

   Ken is trying to (another / approach / persuade / take / them / to) to solving the problem.

E Fill in each blank with a suitable word from the passage. 【思考力・判断力・表現力（内容）】（各 5 点）

1. Aditya is working on problems of (   ) pollution.
2. If we wait for another day to make change, he is not (   ) about the future.
3. His fellow attendees at the Summit are trying to (   ) other people to work toward preventing climate change.

4

Part 4 　教科書 p.11

/52

A　Write the English words to match the Japanese.　【知識・技能（語彙）】（各 2 点）

1. .... 動 所属する A2
2. .... 图 活動家
3. .... 图 率先，主導権 B2
4. .... 图 話，物語 B1
5. .... 图 ごみ，くず B2

B　Choose the word whose underlined part's sound is different from the other three.

【知識・技能（発音）】（各 2 点）

1. ア．activist 　イ．began 　ウ．tale 　エ．track
2. ア．hummingbird 　イ．summit 　ウ．sure 　エ．up
3. ア．activity 　イ．initiative 　ウ．planting 　エ．plastic

C　Complete the following English sentences to match the Japanese.

【知識・技能（表現・文法）】（完答・各 3 点）

1. 私はかつてよく釣りに行っていたものだが，今はしていない。

I (　　　) (　　　) go fishing often, but now I don't.

2. 私の母は家族がいくらのお金を使ったか常に記録を続けている。

My mother always (　　　) (　　　) (　　　) how much money my family spent.

3. 早紀は姉妹校からやって来る生徒を率先して歓迎するだろう。

Saki will (　　　) (　　　) (　　　) in welcoming the students from our sister school.

D　Arrange the words in the proper order to match the Japanese.

【知識・技能（表現・文法）】（各 4 点）

1. 私は常に健康的な生活習慣を心にとめておくようにしている。

I always try to (a / healthy / in / keep / lifestyle / mind).

2. その都市では多くの人々が汚れた空気から身を守るためにマスクをつけている。

Many people in the city wear face masks to (air / from / protect / themselves / unclean).

3. 世界をよりよくするために，今こそ私たち一人ひとりが変化を起こす時なのです。

Now is the time (a change / each / for / make / of / to / us) to make the world better.

E　Fill in each blank with a suitable word from the passage.　【思考力・判断力・表現力（内容）】（各 5 点）

1. Lesein belonged to a (　　　) team and began his "Trees4Goals" activity.
2. Wangari Maathai said, "I will be a (　　　); I will do the best I can."
3. Lesein believes that any little thing we do can (　　　) to save the earth.

Activity Plus

教科書 p.16～p.17

/54

A　Write the English words to match the Japanese.　【知識・技能（語彙）】（各 2 点）

1. _____ 形 模擬の B2
2. _____ 動 …を発生させる B1
3. _____ 形 再生可能な
4. _____ 名 経営陣，理事会 B1
5. _____ 名 経済学 B1
6. _____ 名 知識 A2

B　Choose the word whose stressed syllable is different from the other three.

【知識・技能（発音）】（各 2 点）

1. ア．ap-peal　　　イ．is-sue　　　ウ．knowl-edge　　　エ．wind-mill
2. ア．ac-tiv-ist　　イ．con-vinc-ing　ウ．ex-cel-lent　　エ．gen-er-ate
3. ア．e-co-nom-ics　イ．en-gi-neer-ing　ウ．en-vi-ron-ment　エ．in-for-ma-tion

C　Complete the following English sentences to match the Japanese.

【知識・技能（表現・文法）】（完答・各 3 点）

1. 本を読めば読むほど，人生は幸せになるでしょう。

　　The (　　　　) (　　　　) you read, the (　　　　) your life will be.

2. 若い人たちの中には，インターネットは情報収集の最善の手段だと考える人もいる。

　　(　　　　) young people think that the Internet is the best means of getting information.

3. そんなに怒らないで。落ち着いてお茶でも一杯飲もう。

　　Don't get so angry.　Let's (　　　　) (　　　　) and have a cup of tea.

D　Arrange the words in the proper order to match the Japanese.　【知識・技能（表現・文法）】（各 4 点）

1. この古いタイヤを新しいものに交換しないといけないと思いますよ。

　　I think you have to (a new / old / one / replace / this / tire / with).

2. 私たちの町をよりカーボンニュートラルなものにするために行動を起こしたいと思う活動家を探しています。

　　We are looking for (action / activists / take / to / want / who) to make our town more carbon-neutral.

3. 私のおじは，アフリカでのボランティア活動の知識だけではなく，その経験も持っている。

　　My uncle has experience with (Africa / as / as / in / knowledge / volunteer work / well) of it.

E　Fill in each blank with a suitable word from the passage.　【思考力・判断力・表現力（内容）】（各 5 点）

1. Kazuki read a book about a boy who made a windmill that generates (　　　　).
2. Emily is planning to convince her school's administration to (　　　　) solar panels.
3. Satoshi thinks that his ideas will be more (　　　　) if he has some knowledge about economics.

総合問題

Read the following passage and answer the questions below.

　　The United Nations Youth Climate Summit took place on September 21, 2019. It was held at (A)(in / located / New York / the / UN Headquarters). Young climate action leaders presented their ideas to politicians all over the world. The Youth Climate Summit was followed by the UN Climate Action Summit on September 23.

　　Over 7,000 young people from more than 140 countries and territories applied to the Youth Climate Summit. They were selected (1) the basis of how they worked on climate change and discussed possible solutions. Their performances were evaluated by a panel led by UN officials. After that, 500 of the young people were (B)invite to the Summit. One hundred of them got "Green Tickets." These winners received fully funded travel to New York. Their transportation was (C)(as / as / carbon-neutral / possible). In other words, they used vehicles (2) emitted less carbon dioxide.

　　The participants shared their ideas on the global stage. They delivered a clear message to world leaders: We need to act now to work on climate change.

1.　下線部(A), (C)の（　　　）内の語句を適切に並べかえなさい。　　【知識・技能（文法）】（各5点）

　　(A) ....

　　(C) ....

2.　下線部(B) invite を適切な形に変えなさい。　　【知識・技能（文法）】（4点）

　　（　　　　　　　　　　）

3.　空所(1), (2)に入る適切な語を選びなさい。　　【知識・技能（語彙・表現）】（各5点）

　　(1)　ア．in　　　　　　イ．on　　　　　　ウ．to　　　　　　エ．under

　　(2)　ア．where　　　　イ．which　　　　　ウ．who　　　　　エ．whose

4.　本文の内容に合っているものをすべて選びなさい。　　【思考力・判断力・表現力（内容）】（完答・10点）

　　ア．The Youth Climate Summit was held after the UN Climate Action Summit in 2019.

　　イ．About 140 people applied to the Youth Climate Summit.

　　ウ．A panel led by UN officials evaluated the performances at the Youth Climate Summit.

　　エ．Five hundred young people received fully funded travel to New York.

　　オ．The participants shared their ideas and delivered a message to world leaders.

5.　次の問いの答えになるよう，空所に適切な語を補いなさい。

　　　　【思考力・判断力・表現力（内容）】（完答・各8点）

　　(1)　To whom did young climate action leaders present their ideas?

　　　　── They presented their ideas to (　　　　　) all over the world.

　　(2)　According to the participants' message, what do we need to do to work on climate change? ── We need to (　　　　　) (　　　　　).

ディクテーション

Listen to the English and write down what you hear.

Part 1

You are learning about climate change. On the Internet, you find an article about a high school student who is working on environmentally sustainable (1.　　　　).

Eva Jones, an American (2.　　　　) *student from Hood River Valley High School, attended the United Nations Youth Climate Summit. She was one of the 500 young people selected to join the Summit. She was also one of the 100 "Green Ticket" winners; the United Nations Fund supported her trip to this event.*

I grew up in the Columbia Gorge in the U.S. There are different communities and environments there. I was inspired to be an advocate for the earth and the living things on it.

I'm (3.　　　　) to be selected as a voice at the Summit. Brave action is the only way to make a difference for future generations. We must have our leaders take responsibility seriously.

We have the power to stop the bad (4.　　　　) that are changing the earth's climate. The main way is to use our money for encouraging sustainable consumption and for stopping the use of unclean energy. I'm proud to (5.　　　　) my lovely hometown and the environmental beauty I grew up in.

Part 2

Climate change is one of the biggest environmental problems. These days, the need to deal with it is becoming increasingly (1.　　　　).

① The United Nations Youth Climate Summit took place on September 21, 2019. It was held at the UN Headquarters (2.　　　　) in New York. Young climate action leaders presented their ideas to politicians all over the world. The Youth Climate Summit was followed by the UN Climate Action Summit on September 23.

② Over 7,000 young people from more than 140 countries and territories applied to the Youth Climate Summit. They were selected on the basis of how they worked on climate change and discussed possible solutions. Their performances were (3.　　　　) by a panel led by UN officials. After that, 500 of the young people were invited to the Summit. One hundred of them got "Green Tickets." These winners received fully funded travel to New York. Their transportation was as carbon-neutral as possible. In other words, they used (4.　　　　) which emitted less carbon dioxide.

③ The (5.　　　　) shared their ideas on the global stage. They delivered a clear message to world leaders: We need to act now to work on climate change.

Part 3

④ One of the participants at the Summit was 15-year-old Aditya Mukarji from India. He is working on problems of plastic pollution.

⑤ In India, Aditya helps an NGO so that businesses can (1.　　　　) their waste and recycle plastics. He also promotes the use of more eco-friendly goods than plastics. For example, at the age of 13, Aditya went to cafés and restaurants, (2.　　　　) them to use eco-friendly alternatives instead of plastic straws and other single-use plastics. He said, "I'm (3.   ) about the future if we can make change today. If we wait for another day, I'm not." He is promoting the philosophy of "(4.   ) If You Cannot Reuse."

⑥ Aditya was impressed by his fellow attendees at the Summit. "All these youths who come here are excellent in their fields. They are all the best, and they are trying to empower other people to work toward (5.   ) climate change," he said. "They all have the same ideal: to save the earth. They all have different approaches."

Part 4

⑦ Fifteen-year-old Lesein Mathenge Mutunkei from Kenya also joined the Summit. He (1.   ) to a soccer team and began his "Trees4Goals" activity in 2018. "I used to plant one tree for every goal I scored. But now I plant 11 trees for every goal," said Lesein. He has planted more than 1,400 trees. He also keeps track of the places where he planted the trees so that he can make sure that they are growing.

⑧ Lesein respects Wangari Maathai, a Kenyan environmental (2.   ). She took the initiative in planting trees in Africa. He always keeps her words in mind: "I will be a hummingbird; I will do the best I can." In an Ecuadorean folk (3.   ), only the little hummingbird tried to protect the forest from a big fire.

⑨ Lesein wants to learn new ways to help save the planet. "Maathai did her part, and now it is time for young people to do their part. Any little thing we do can be a help. Planting a tree, picking up (4.   ), or even sharing information on the Internet … everything counts," he says.

Activity Plus

In an English class, a teacher and three students are speaking at a mock youth climate summit. You are listening to them.

Teacher: Here we have three excellent climate activists. Now, please share your actions for protecting the environment. Will you start, Kazuki?

Kazuki: Well, I'm interested in engineering. I read a book about an African boy who made a windmill that (1.   ) electricity. We need renewable energy sources to replace generators which use fossil fuels.

Teacher: So, Kazuki, you believe that we must replace fossil fuels with more eco-friendly energy sources. Next, can you tell us what you're doing, Emily?

Emily: I'm planning to write a letter to (2.   ) our school's administration to install solar panels. I started looking for supporters and have found teachers and friends who agree with my idea. The more supporters I have, the stronger my (3.   ) will become.

Teacher: Thank you, Emily! You're saying that finding more supporters for your idea is the key. Satoshi, how about you? What action are you taking?

Satoshi: I started studying economics as well as environmental issues. Some world leaders are saying that young activists should calm down and study (4.   ) first. If I have some knowledge about economics, my ideas about environmental issues will be more convincing.

Teacher: I see, Satoshi. Your point is that it is important to make your opinion (5.   ).

Part 1 　教科書 p.22〜p.23　　／54

A Write the English words to match the Japanese.　【知識・技能（語彙）】（各2点）

1. .... 图 生活様式，生き方 A2　　2. .... 副 滅多に…ない B2
3. .... 動 降りる B2　　4. .... 图 舌 B1
5. .... 動 伸びる B1　　6. .... 图 枝 A2

B Choose the word whose underlined part's sound is different from the other three.

【知識・技能（発音）】（各2点）

1. ア．c<u>a</u>ge　　イ．c<u>a</u>re　　ウ．<u>e</u>ntrance　　エ．ext<u>e</u>nd
2. ア．<u>al</u>most　　イ．b<u>al</u>l　　ウ．br<u>a</u>nch　　エ．s<u>al</u>t
3. ア．gr<u>ou</u>nd　　イ．gr<u>ow</u>　　ウ．m<u>ou</u>th　　エ．t<u>ow</u>n

C Complete the following English sentences to match the Japanese.

【知識・技能（表現・文法）】（完答・各3点）

1. 彼は都会で一人暮らしをしていたとき，滅多に母親に手紙を書かなかった。

   He (　　　　) wrote to his mother when he lived (　　　　) (　　　　) (　　　　)
   in a city.

2. 私はほとんどいつも一日に10キロ走る。

   I (　　　　) (　　　　) run 10 kilometers (　　　　) (　　　　).

3. その母親は公園で子供たちから決して目を離さなかった。

   The mother (　　　　) took her eyes (　　　　) her children in the park.

D Arrange the words in the proper order to match the Japanese.

【知識・技能（表現・文法）】（各4点）

1. 彼はプレゼンテーションの準備でずっと忙しい。

   He (been / busy / for / has / his presentation / preparing).

2. この洗濯機は一度に7キロまで洗濯物を洗うことができる。

   This washing machine can wash (a / at / laundry / of / time / to / up / 7 kg).

3. 父は私の倍の本を持っている。

   My father has (as / as / books / do / I / many / twice).

E Fill in each blank with a suitable word from the passage.

【思考力・判断力・表現力（内容）】（完答・各5点）

1. Animal No.1 only eats the leaves of a (　　　　) tree.
2. Animal No.2 has to eat a (　　　　) (　　　　) of leaves every day.
3. Animal No.3 makes a bed with branches it takes (　　　　) trees.

10

Part 2　教科書 p.24

 /54

A　Write the English words to match the Japanese.　【知識・技能（語彙）】（各 2 点）

1. _____ 動 異なる，違う B1　　2. _____ 副 たいていは A2
3. _____ 名 含有量，容量 B1　　4. _____ 名 栄養，栄養物 B1
5. _____ 名 毒素　　6. _____ 前 …以外に，…を除いて B1

B　Choose the word whose stressed syllable is different from the other three.

【知識・技能（発音）】（各 2 点）

1.　ア．a-round　　　イ．con-tain　　　ウ．gi-raffe　　　エ．life-style
2.　ア．an-i-mal　　　イ．en-er-gy　　　ウ．gen-er-al　　　エ．ko-a-la
3.　ア．con-vinc-ing　イ．how-ev-er　　ウ．spe-cif-ic　　エ．var-i-ous

C　Complete the following English sentences to match the Japanese.

【知識・技能（表現・文法）】（完答・各 3 点）

1.　一般に，男の子は電車や車が好きだ。

(　　　　) (　　　　　), little boys like trains and cars.

2.　健康でいるために，私はバランスの取れた食事をしている。

To stay (　　　　), I eat a balanced (　　　　).

3.　例えば AI 業界では，1,000 の仕事が生まれた。

In the AI industry, (　　　　) (　　　　　), 1,000 jobs have been created.

D　Arrange the words in the proper order to match the Japanese.

【知識・技能（表現・文法）】（各 4 点）

1.　金メダルを取るために，彼は大きな努力をした。

He made (a / effort / great / in / order / to / win) a gold medal.

2.　ストレスを解消するために，私はよく海を見に行きます。

I often (get / go / of / rid / see / the ocean / to / to) my stress.

3.　その城は王妃のために建てられたと考えられている。

It is (built / for / that / the castle / thought / was) the queen.

E　Fill in each blank with a suitable word from the passage.

【思考力・判断力・表現力（内容）】（完答・各 5 点）

1. Sleeping time (　　　　) greatly (　　　　) animal to animal. For instance, koalas sleep for about 20 hours a day, but giraffes sleep for only about 2 hours.
2. Eucalyptus leaves have a high water (　　　　) but are poor in (　　　　).
3. Koalas can (　　　　) (　　　　) (　　　　) toxins eucalyptus leaves contain.

Part 3 教科書 p.25

A Write the English words to match the Japanese.　【知識・技能 (語彙)】(各 2 点)

1. .... 图 対照, 対比 A2　　2. .... 動 …を維持する, 保つ B1
3. .... 图 哺乳類　　4. .... 图 肉食動物, 捕食動物
5. .... 图 ヒョウ B2　　6. .... 图 タンパク質

B Choose the word whose underlined part's sound is different from the other three.

【知識・技能 (発音)】(各 2 点)

1. ア. mostly　　イ. only　　ウ. total　　エ. toxin
2. ア. action　　イ. land　　ウ. stand　　エ. vary
3. ア. besides　　イ. feeding　　ウ. leaves　　エ. these

C Complete the following English sentences to match the Japanese.

【知識・技能 (表現・文法)】(完答・各 3 点)

1. 国の北部とは対照的に, ここは温暖な気候だ。

  (　　　) (　　　) (　　　　) the northern part of the country, this place has a mild climate.

2. 可能なら, 窓側の席を取りたいです。

  I would like to have a window seat (　　　) (　　　).

3. 合計で62名がミーティングに出席した。

  (　　　) (　　　　), 62 people attended the meeting.

D Arrange the words in the proper order to match the Japanese.

【知識・技能 (表現・文法)】(各 4 点)

1. この映画はあの映画よりもずっと面白い。

  This movie (far / interesting / is / more / than / that).

2. その自動車メーカーの作る車は, スタイリッシュなデザインに進化した。

  The cars (evolved / have / into / makes / that / the automaker) stylish designs.

3. 多くの人がそのランニングシューズに500ドルも支払った。

  Many people (as / as / for / much / paid / 500 dollars) the running shoes.

E Fill in each blank with a suitable word from the passage.

【思考力・判断力・表現力 (内容)】(完答・各 5 点)

1. Giraffes mostly stand (　　　) sleeping.
2. It takes many hours (　　　) grazing animals (　　　) eat a lot of leaves and grass.
3. The food meat-eating animals have contains lots of (　　　).

Part 4　教科書 p.28

/54

A　Write the English words to match the Japanese.　【知識・技能（語彙）】（各2点）

1. ....　動 呼吸する A1
2. ....　名 半球
3. ....　副 交替に
4. ....　形 停止中の
5. ....　名 行動 A2
6. ....　形 数えきれないほどの B1

B　Choose the word whose stressed syllable is different from the other three.

【知識・技能（発音）】（各2点）

1. ア．dol-phin　　イ．mod-ern　　ウ．re-peat　　エ．sur-face
2. ア．con-trast　　イ．leop-ard　　ウ．main-tain　　エ．there-fore
3. ア．be-hav-ior　　イ．de-vel-op　　ウ．nu-tri-tious　　エ．pred-a-tor

C　Complete the following English sentences to match the Japanese.

【知識・技能（表現・文法）】（完答・各3点）

1. 彼はその解決策を完全に彼自身で発見した。

   He discovered the solution (　　　　) by himself.
2. 最近，燃料の価格が上昇している。同様に，食料品の価格も上昇しつつある。

   Recently, the price of fuel has been rising. (　　　　), food prices are also rising.
3. 遠くから見ると，その島はハート型に見える。

   (　　　) (　　　　) a distance, the island looks heart-shaped.

D　Arrange the words in the proper order to match the Japanese.

【知識・技能（表現・文法）】（各4点）

1. 私たちが明日までにこの作業を終えることは不可能だ。

   It is (by / finish / for / impossible / this work / to / us) tomorrow.

   ....
2. 人間は火を使うことができるという点で動物と違う。

   Human beings (animals / differ / from / in / that) they can use fire.

   ....
3. ひとさじのはちみつが，そのスープをおいしくした。

   A spoonful (delicious / honey / made / of / the soup).

   ....

E　Fill in each blank with a suitable word from the passage.

【思考力・判断力・表現力（内容）】（完答・各5点）

1. Some marine (　　　　), such as whales and dolphins, have different sleeping styles.
2. During slow-wave activity, the (　　　　) of a dolphin's brain sleep alternately.
3. Affected (　　　　) their living environments, all animals on the (　　　　) have developed different sleep behaviors.

13

Activity Plus 教科書 p.32〜p.33

A Write the English words to match the Japanese. 【知識・技能（語彙）】（各2点）

1. _____ 图 専門家 A2
2. _____ 圖 全般的に，一般に B1
3. _____ 形 平均の A2
4. _____ 图 疲れ
5. _____ 图 不足 B1
6. _____ 图 肥満

B Choose the word whose underlined part's sound is different from the other three.

【知識・技能（発音）】（各2点）

1. ア. ad<u>u</u>lt   イ. b<u>a</u>d   ウ. c<u>o</u>me   エ. n<u>u</u>mber
2. ア. ba<u>th</u>   イ. brea<u>the</u>   ウ. heal<u>th</u>y   エ. <u>th</u>ousand
3. ア. d<u>i</u>et   イ. l<u>i</u>e   ウ. r<u>i</u>sk   エ. wh<u>i</u>le

C Complete the following English sentences to match the Japanese.

【知識・技能（表現・文法）】（完答・各3点）

1. 私はある政治家に質問する機会があった。

   I had an opportunity to (　　　　) questions (　　　　) a politician.
2. そのデータを見せながら，医者は喫煙のリスクを説明した。

   The doctor explained the risks of smoking, (　　　) (　　　) (　　　).
3. 天気予報によると，今週末に雪が降るだろう。

   (　　　) (　　　　) the weather forecast, it will snow this weekend.

D Arrange the words in the proper order to match the Japanese.

【知識・技能（表現・文法）】（各4点）

1. 喫煙者の数はこの10年間で減ってきている。

   The (been / decreasing / has / number / of / over / smokers) the past decade.

   ----
2. 食べ過ぎは私たちの健康に悪い。

   (bad / eating / for / is / much / our health / too).

   ----
3. 車で1時間弱で，私たちは森に着いた。

   (an / drive / hour's / less / than / took) us to the forest.

E Fill in each blank with a suitable word from the passage.

【思考力・判断力・表現力（内容）】（完答・各5点）

1. Graph 1 shows that the (　　　　) (　　　) time of Japanese adults is getting (　　　　).
2. The expert says that sleep helps us get rid of our (　　　　).
3. People who sleep longer than (　　　　) hours a day have a higher (　　　　) of death, too.

総合問題

Read the following passage and answer the questions below.

　Some marine mammals, such (1) whales and dolphins, have different sleeping styles. They have to come regularly up to the surface of the sea to breathe. It is (A)(both / for / impossible / sleep / them / to / with) their brains and their bodies resting entirely. They have to keep swimming and breathing while (B)sleep.

　Dolphins are unique (2) that they keep one brain hemisphere in slow-wave activity while they sleep. During slow-wave activity, the hemispheres of a dolphin's brain sleep (C)alternate, and they each sleep for only a short time. The left hemisphere is sleeping while the right eye is closed. Similarly, the right hemisphere is inactive while the left eye is closed. The dolphins repeat (D)this behavior countless times while they are sleeping.

　(E)Affect by their living environments, all animals on the globe have (F)develop different sleep behaviors and different sleeping hours. Their lifestyles are the results (3) evolution and specialization. Research (G)(animal / clear / facts / has / interesting / made / many / on / sleep) to us.

---

1. 空所(1), (2), (3)に入る適切な語を書きなさい。　　　　　【知識・技能（語彙）】（各4点）

　　(1) ....　(2) ....　(3) ....

2. 下線部(A), (G)の（　　）内の語を適切に並べかえなさい。　　【知識・技能（表現・文法）】（各5点）

　　(A) ....

　　(G) ....

3. 下線部(B), (C), (E), (F)の語を適切な形に変えなさい。　　　【知識・技能（文法）】（各4点）

　　(B) (　　　　　)　　(C) (　　　　　)　　(E) (　　　　　)　　(F) (　　　　　)

4. 下線部(D)が指す内容を日本語で説明しなさい。　　　【思考力・判断力・表現力（内容）】（5点）

　　..

5. 次の問いの答えになるよう，空所に適切な語を補いなさい。　【思考力・判断力・表現力（内容）】（5点）

　　What do whales and dolphins have to do while they are sleeping?

　　――They have to keep (　　　　　) and come up to the surface of the sea to (　　　　　) regularly.

15

ディクテーション

Listen to the English and write down what you hear.

Part 1

You and your friend are visiting a zoo. At the entrance, you are given a picture card which shows the (1.   ) of three animals. On the card, each animal asks you to guess what animal it is.

Who Am I?

The answer to each "Who Am I?" question is in front of our cages. Please come and see us!

Animal No.1: I almost always live in a tree and (2.   ) descend to the ground. I only eat the leaves of a specific tree, and I usually don't drink water. I don't like moving around, but I like sleeping very much. I sleep about 20 hours a day. Who am I?

Animal No.2: I am very tall, and I like eating the leaves of tall trees. I have to eat a large amount of leaves every day. My (3.   ) can extend up to 50 centimeters out of my mouth, so I can take many leaves off a branch at a time. I only sleep about two hours a day because I am busy eating. Who am I?

Animal No.3: The (4.   ) is my home and I never go down to the ground. I don't have a family, and I live all by myself. I have long arms that are about twice as long as my legs. My favorite food is fruit. I make a bed to sleep in with branches I take from trees. Who am I?

Part 2

How long do animals sleep? Do most animals sleep as long as human beings do every day?

1 In (1.   ), human beings need seven to eight hours of sleep every night in order to stay healthy. This means that we spend about one third of our whole life sleeping. However, what about other animals? Sleeping time (2.   ) greatly from animal to animal. For instance, koalas sleep for about 20 hours a day, but giraffes' sleeping time is amazingly short——only about two hours a day.

2 Koalas (3.   ) live in trees, and they feed, sleep or rest most of the time. They eat only eucalyptus leaves. The leaves have a high water (4.   ) but are poor in nutrition. Therefore, koalas don't get enough energy from their diet to move around much.

3 Eucalyptus leaves also contain (5.   ) that are hard for other animals to remove. Koalas can get rid of these toxins, but it takes a lot of energy to do that. It is thought that they save energy by doing nothing (6.   ) eating and resting.

Part 3

4 In contrast to koalas, giraffes sleep only for short periods of time. (1.   ) research shows that giraffes usually sleep only about two hours a day in total. They mostly stand while sleeping, and they lie down on the ground to sleep for only a few minutes. Giraffes are the tallest land animals, and they need to eat a huge amount of

leaves every day to (2.   ) their large bodies. They have to spend far more time feeding than sleeping.

5   Most large (3.   ) mammals, such as giraffes, horses and elephants, are short-sleepers. It takes many hours for these animals to eat a lot of leaves or grass. It is thought that they evolved into short-sleepers because they needed to reduce the danger of being attacked by (4.   ) like lions, leopards and hyenas.

6   Meat-eating animals, on the other hand, sleep as much as 13 to 15 hours a day. Their food contains lots of protein, so it is very (5.   ). Therefore, they don't have to spend a great amount of time feeding.

Part 4

7   Some marine mammals, such as whales and dolphins, have different sleeping styles. They have to come (1.   ) up to the surface of the sea to breathe. It is impossible for them to sleep with both their brains and their bodies resting (2.   ). They have to keep swimming and breathing while sleeping.

8   Dolphins are unique in that they keep one brain (3.   ) in slow-wave activity while they sleep. During slow-wave activity, the hemispheres of a dolphin's brain sleep (4.   ), and they each sleep for only a short time. The left hemisphere is sleeping while the right eye is closed. Similarly, the right hemisphere is inactive while the left eye is closed. The dolphins repeat this (5.   ) countless times while they are sleeping.

9   Affected by their living environments, all animals on the globe have developed different sleep behaviors and different sleeping hours. Their lifestyles are the results of evolution and (6.   ). Research on animal sleep has made many interesting facts clear to us.

Activity Plus

A Japanese high school student asks some questions of an (1.   ) who studies human sleep. The expert answers the student, showing graphs.

Student: Do you think Japanese people (2.   ) get enough sleep?

  Expert: According to a recent survey, the (3.   ) sleeping time of Japanese adults is getting shorter. As Graph 1 shows, the number of people who sleep less than six hours every day has been increasing, and the number of people getting more than seven hours of sleep has been decreasing.

Student: What's the purpose of sleep? What is important about sleep?

  Expert: Sleep helps us get rid of our (4.   ). It is also important for refreshing our brain and keeping it healthy. A shortage of sleep is bad for our health, and it increases our risk of (5.   ) and heart disease. Eventually, it raises our risk of death.

Student: Is it better for us to sleep as long as we can to stay healthy?

  Expert: Sleeping too long may not be better for us. One interesting fact we have learned from studies is that those who sleep longer than eight hours a day have a higher risk of death, too, like short-sleepers. Graph 2 shows that people who sleep around seven hours a day have the (6.   ) risk of death.

A　Write the English words to match the Japanese.　【知識・技能 (語彙)】(各 2 点)

1. .... 图 勝利，優勝 B1
2. .... 形 感謝する A2
3. .... 形 大きな，巨大な B1
4. .... 图 困難 B1
5. .... 图 感謝 (の気持ち) B1
6. .... 图 審判員

B　Choose the word whose stressed syllable is different from the other three.

【知識・技能 (発音)】(各 2 点)

1. ア．con-sump-tion　イ．grat-i-tude　ウ．head-quar-ters　エ．ve-hi-cle
2. ア．ac-knowl-edge　イ．in-ju-ry　ウ．op-po-nent　エ．sin-cere-ly
3. ア．a-chieve-ment　イ．fre-quent-ly　ウ．or-gan-ize　エ．prob-a-bly

C　Complete the following English sentences to match the Japanese.

【知識・技能 (表現・文法)】(完答・各 3 点)

1. 大谷翔平が記録を更新したとき，観衆は彼に声援を送った。

   The crowd (　　　　) (　　　　　　) Shohei Otani when he broke the record.
2. 私たちはアメリカと対戦します。

   We play a (　　　　) (　　　　) America.
3. この賞をいただいて大変光栄です。

   I (　　　　) (　　　　　) to be awarded this prize.

D　Arrange the words in the proper order to match the Japanese.

【知識・技能 (表現・文法)】(各 4 点)

1. 私たちはみなさんに感謝しています。

   We would (express / like / thanks / to / to / you all).

   ----
2. 彼女はたくさんの困難を経験した。

   She (a lot of / experienced / hardship / has) in life.

   ----
3. 文化祭の成功の背景には生徒たちの協力があった。

   There was (behind / from / support / the students / the success) of the school festival.

E　Fill in each blank with a suitable word from the passage.

【思考力・判断力・表現力 (内容)】(各 5 点)

1. We listen to Naomi's speech after her final match (　　　　) Serena Williams.
2. Naomi was (　　　　) to play with Petra Kvitová in the final.
3. (　　　　) though it was hot, many people still came to show support.

A Write the English words to match the Japanese.　【知識・技能（語彙）】（各2点）

1. _____ 動 …を引き付ける B1　　2. _____ 形 心からの B2

3. _____ 名 謙遜　　4. _____ 動 …を称賛する B2

5. _____ 動 …を克服する B1　　6. _____ 名 負傷, けが B1

B Choose the word whose underlined part's sound is different from the other three.　【知識・技能（発音）】（各2点）

1. ア. attr<u>a</u>ct　　イ. pr<u>ai</u>se　　ウ. st<u>a</u>ff　　エ. tr<u>a</u>vel

2. ア. h<u>u</u>mble　　イ. <u>i</u>njury　　ウ. sl<u>u</u>mp　　エ. <u>u</u>mpire

3. ア. aw<u>ar</u>d　　イ. <u>or</u>ganize　　ウ. sh<u>or</u>tage　　エ. w<u>or</u>d

C Complete the following English sentences to match the Japanese.　【知識・技能（表現・文法）】（各3点）

1. 彼らが勝とうが負けようが，大した問題ではない。

It doesn't matter (　　　) they win or lose.

2. あなたはこれらの問題を一つずつ片付ける必要がある。

You need to solve these problems one (　　　) one.

3. 彼は私と視線を合わせようとしなかった。

He didn't try to keep eye (　　　) with me.

D Arrange the words in the proper order to match the Japanese.　【知識・技能（表現・文法）】（各4点）

1. 私たちは，人々を魅了する観光地を紹介します。

We will (attract / introduce / people / that / the sight-seeing spots / to / you).

2. 選手にとって対戦相手の努力を評価することは大切です。

It is (acknowledge / athletes / for / important / their opponents' hard work / to).

3. 彼女には息子が3人おり，みんな同じ会社で働いています。

She (all / has / in the same office / three sons, / who / work).

E Fill in each blank with a suitable word from the passage.　【表現力・判断力・思考力（内容）】（完答・各5点）

1. Petra Kvitová had been (　　　) hardships.

2. Naomi sincerely (　　　) her opponent.

3. The opponents had to overcome some difficulties, (　　　) (　　　) injuries or slumps.

Part 3 　教科書 p.41

A　Write the English words to match the Japanese.　【知識・技能 (語彙)】(各 2 点)

1. ＿＿＿＿＿＿＿　图 栄養士
2. ＿＿＿＿＿＿＿　動 …を組織する A2
3. ＿＿＿＿＿＿＿　動 …を負かす B1
4. ＿＿＿＿＿＿＿　图 賞, 賞金 A2
5. ＿＿＿＿＿＿＿　图 式, 式典 B1
6. ＿＿＿＿＿＿＿　图 団体 B1

B　Choose the word whose stressed syllable is different from the other three.

【知識・技能 (発音)】(各 2 点)

1. ア. grat-i-tude　　イ. in-ju-ry　　ウ. in-ter-view　　エ. sup-port-er
2. ア. at-tract　　イ. de-feat　　ウ. en-tire　　エ. spon-sor
3. ア. op-po-nent　　イ. o-ver-come　　ウ. sin-cere-ly　　エ. to-geth-er

C　Complete the following English sentences to match the Japanese.

【知識・技能 (表現・文法)】(各 3 点)

1. 私たちは全員リーダーに投票しました。

   We all (　　　　) for our leader.
2. あなたが手伝ってくれなければ, 私たちの仕事は成功しないでしょう。

   If you (　　　　) help us, our work (　　　　) be successful.
3. 彼はスピーチで自分の国に対する感謝を表した。

   He expressed his (　　　　) to his country in his speech.

D　Arrange the words in the proper order to match the Japanese.

【知識・技能 (表現・文法)】(各 4 点)

1. 私は, 人々がいつも私を支えてくれることに感謝しています。

   I (am / for / grateful / me / people / supporting / to) all the time.

   ＿＿＿＿＿＿＿＿＿＿＿＿＿＿＿＿＿＿＿＿＿＿＿＿＿
2. たくさんの人が彼が参加した競技に関わっていた。

   Many people (concerned / he / joined / the sports event / were / with).

   ＿＿＿＿＿＿＿＿＿＿＿＿＿＿＿＿＿＿＿＿＿＿＿＿＿
3. この仕事をするには, 健康と忍耐力は欠かせない。

   (and / are / essential / health / patience / this job / to do).

   ＿＿＿＿＿＿＿＿＿＿＿＿＿＿＿＿＿＿＿＿＿＿＿＿＿

E　Fill in each blank with a suitable word from the passage.

【思考力・判断力・表現力 (内容)】(各 5 点)

1. They are working together as a team. (　　　　) them, many staff members are essential.
2. Siya Kolisi said to people in his country, "I cannot thank you (　　　　)."
3. They were the people (　　　　) the great event.

Part 4 教科書 p.42

/54

A Write the English words to match the Japanese. 　【知識・技能（語彙）】（各2点）

1. .... 图 手法, テクニック B1　　2. .... 副 わざと, 故意に B1

3. .... 形 好意的な B1　　4. .... 形 謙虚な B2

5. .... 副 できれば B1　　6. .... 形 優秀な B1

B Choose the word whose underlined part's sound is different from the other three.

【知識・技能（発音）】（各2点）

1. ア. an<u>a</u>lyze　　イ. congr<u>a</u>ts　　ウ. f<u>a</u>vorable　　エ. gr<u>a</u>titude

2. ア. ent<u>i</u>re　　イ. nutr<u>i</u>tionist　　ウ. s<u>i</u>ncere　　エ. v<u>i</u>ctory

3. ア. h<u>o</u>pefully　　イ. <u>o</u>pponent　　ウ. <u>o</u>vercome　　エ. pr<u>o</u>bably

C Complete the following English sentences to match the Japanese.

【知識・技能（表現・文法）】（完答・各3点）

1. 彼女はオーストラリアで生まれたと言ったが, それは本当ではなかった。

She said that she was born in Australia, (　　　　) was not true.

2. その俳優は病気のせいで観客に感銘を与えることができなかった。

The actor failed to make an (　　　　) (　　　　) the audience because he was ill.

3. 彼はたまたま, ちょうどよいときに来た。

He happened to come at (　　　　) (　　　　) time.

D Arrange the words in the proper order to match the Japanese.

【知識・技能（表現・文法）】（各4点）

1. この音楽はあなたを気分よくさせるでしょう。

This music (better / feel / make / will / you).

....

2. あの赤い帽子をかぶっている女性は私の妹です。

The woman (a red hat / is / is wearing / my sister / who).

....

3. 次に彼女が来るのは今度の金曜日です。

(comes / is / she / the next time) this Friday.

....

E Fill in each blank with a suitable word from the passage.

【思考力・判断力・表現力（内容）】（各5点）

1. You can become a speaker who is (　　　　) to your audience.

2. Shohei Otani finished his speech (　　　　) the following sentences.

3. Being (　　　　) is difficult, but athletes often use this technique in their speeches.

21

Activity Plus 　教科書 p.48〜p.49 　／54

A　Write the English words to match the Japanese.　【知識・技能 (語彙)】(各2点)

1. _____ 圏 おめでとう　　　2. _____ 動 競争する, 争う B1

3. _____ 名 観客, 見物人 B1　　4. _____ 名 雰囲気 B1

5. _____ 名 遊び場 A2　　　　6. _____ 名 事態, 状況 A2

B　Choose the word whose stressed syllable is different from the other three.

【知識・技能 (語彙)】(各2点)

1. ア. ac-knowl-edge　　イ. at-mos-phere　　ウ. im-pres-sion　　エ. out-stand-ing

2. ア. com-pete　　　　イ. grate-ful　　　　ウ. per-fect　　　　エ. play-ground

3. ア. con-grat-u-la-tion　　　　　　イ. ex-am-i-na-tion
　 ウ. in-ten-tion-al-ly　　　　　　エ. or-gan-i-za-tion

C　Complete the following English sentences to match the Japanese.

【知識・技能 (表現・文法)】(完答・各3点)

1. 卒業おめでとう。

　 (　　　　) (　　　　) your graduation.

2. もしあなたが助けてくれなかったら，私は成功しなかっただろう。

　 If you (　　　　) (　　　　) me, I couldn't have succeeded.

3. 家でテレビを見ていた妹は，私に何があったか理解していなかった。

　 My sister, (　　　　) TV at home, didn't understand what had happened to me.

D　Arrange the words in the proper order to match the Japanese.

【知識・技能 (表現・文法)】(各4点)

1. 友達と楽しい時間を過ごしていることを願ってるよ。

　 I (a good time / are / having / hope / with / you) your friends.

2. 試合のために練習しないといけなかった日は本当にきつかった。

　 The days (for / had to / I / practice / the match / were / when) really hard.

3. 彼はその賞のために3人の相手と競い合った。

　 He (competed / for / opponents / the prize / three / with).

E　Fill each blank with a suitable word from the passage.

【思考力・判断力・表現力 (内容)】(各5点)

1. Roger was so grateful (　　　　) his family for supporting him.

2. The center court was (　　　　) with a lot of spectators.

3. It was a great time for Roger to be able to compete (　　　　) Marin.

総合問題

/50

Read the following passage and answer the questions below.

Finally, (A)(a technique / humility / is / quite / showing / unique) to the speeches of professional athletes.　They intentionally confess their worries or weaknesses in their speeches, (1) hurts no one and makes a favorable impression (2) listeners.　Being humble can be difficult, but athletes often use this technique in their speeches.

At the awards ceremony for Rookie of the Year, Shohei Otani was holding his notes for his speech.　He looked down at them frequently during his speech.　(3), he finished his speech with the sentence, "Hopefully, I will not need this cheat sheet the next time I'm up here."　Showing humility made his audience (4) at just the right time.

You can learn (B)(athletes / by / looking / professional / think / what) at these four special features in their victory speeches.　When you deliver a speech in English, you can use some of these techniques to make your speech more impressive.　If you analyze athletes' outstanding speeches, you too can become a speaker who is attractive to your audience.

1.　空所(1), (2), (3), (4)に入る適切な語を選びなさい。　　【知識・技能（語彙・表現）】（各4点）

   (1)　ア．but　　　　　イ．that　　　　　ウ．which　　　　エ．who
   (2)　ア．at　　　　　イ．in　　　　　　ウ．of　　　　　エ．on
   (3)　ア．Also　　　　イ．Fortunately　　ウ．However　　　エ．Therefore
   (4)　ア．laugh　　　　イ．laughed　　　　ウ．laughing　　　エ．to laugh

2.　下線部(A), (B)の（　　　）内の語句を適切に並べかえなさい。　　【知識・技能（文法）】（各5点）

   (A) ---

   (B) ---

3.　本文の内容に合っているものをすべて選びなさい。　　【思考力・判断力・表現力（内容）】（完答・8点）

   ア．Shohei Otani said that he would not use a cheat sheet for his speech next time.
   イ．Being humble can be so difficult that few athletes use this technique in their speeches.
   ウ．At the end of his speech, Shohei confessed that he had looked down at his notes.
   エ．You can be a good speaker if you analyze athletes' outstanding speeches.
   オ．Professional athletes don't want to confess their worries or weaknesses in their speeches.

4.　次の問いの答えになるよう，空所に適切な語を補いなさい。【思考力・判断力・表現力（内容）】（完答・各8点）

   (1)　What is one of the techniques in the speeches that attract people?
   　　── (　　　　　) (　　　　　) is.

   (2)　What was Shohei doing at the awards ceremony for Rookie of the Year?
   　　── He was holding his (　　　　　) for his (　　　　　).

23

ディクテーション

Listen to the English and write down what you hear.

Part 1

You found two short video clips of tennis player Naomi Osaka's ($_1$.   ) speeches on the Internet. You are watching them.

A: Naomi's speech after her final match against Serena Williams (USA) in the 2018 U.S. Open Championships

　I know that everyone was cheering for Serena Williams, and I'm sorry our final match had to end like this. I'd just like to thank all of you for coming and watching this match.

　It was always my dream to play with Serena in the U.S. Open finals. So I'm glad that I was able to do that, and I'm ($_2$.   ) I was able to play with her. Thank you!

B: Naomi's speech after her final match against Petra Kvitová (the Czech Republic) in the 2019 Australian Open Championships

　Huge ($_3$.   ) to you, Petra, and your team! I've always wanted to play with you. And you've been through hardships. You're really amazing. I was honored to play with you in the final.

　Even though it's very hot, many people still came to show support, so I want to show my ($_4$.   ) to them, too. So, thanks to Craig, the tournament director, the ball kids running around in the heat, the ($_5$.   ), the volunteers, everyone. They make this tournament possible, so I want to thank them all, too. And thanks to my team. There is always a team behind a tennis player.

Part 2

Professional athletes around the world often make a victory speech in English. Their speeches have some features in common. What are they?

1 What do athletes tell people in their victory speeches after the competition is over? You can find four features in their speeches that ($_1$.   ) people. They are: to honor their opponents, to acknowledge their opponents' achievements, to express their sincere thanks, and to show ($_2$.   ). Let's check each feature one by one.

2 First, it is important for athletes to ($_3$.   ) their opponents at the beginning of their speeches. They usually keep eye contact with their opponents. For example, Naomi Osaka, who won the final match of the 2018 U.S. Open Championships, sincerely honored her opponent, Serena Williams. Serena also did that in her speech. It doesn't matter ($_4$.   ) they win or lose.

3 Second, many winners acknowledge their opponents' hard work. Their opponents probably had to ($_5$.   ) some difficulties before the tournament, such as injuries, slumps or frustrations. For example, in the 2019 Australian Open Championships, Naomi said to her opponent, Petra Kvitová, "You've been through hardships."

Part 3

4 Third, players often thank all of their fans and supporters. There are always coaches, teammates, trainers, managers and nutritionists behind a professional athlete. They are all working together as a team. Besides them, many ($_1$.   ) members, such as judges, officials, sponsors and ball kids, are essential to ($_2$.   ) a tournament. If these people did not support athletes, there couldn't be a tournament.

⑤ In the 2019 Rugby World Cup in Japan, South Africa (3.   ) England in the final game. Siya Kolisi, who was the captain, expressed his gratitude to his own country, South Africa, in his victory interview.　He said to people in his country, "I cannot thank you enough.　I'm so grateful to all the people in South Africa for cheering for us."

⑥ The baseball player Shohei Otani was named Rookie of the Year in 2018.　In his speech at the awards ceremony, he thanked all the people (4.   ) with the award he received.　They were the people hosting the great event, the baseball writers voting for him, the (5.   ) Angels organization, his fans, and his parents.

Part 4

⑦ Finally, showing humility is a technique quite unique to the speeches of professional athletes.　They intentionally (1.   ) their worries or weaknesses in their speeches, which hurts no one and makes a favorable impression on listeners. Being (2.   ) can be difficult, but athletes often use this technique in their speeches.

⑧ At the awards ceremony for Rookie of the Year, Shohei Otani was holding his notes for his speech.　He looked down at them (3.   ) during his speech.　However, he finished his speech with the sentence, "Hopefully, I will not need this cheat sheet the next time I'm up here."　Showing humility made his (4.   ) laugh at just the right time.

⑨ You can learn what professional athletes think by looking at these four special features in their victory speeches.　When you deliver a speech in English, you can use some of these techniques to make your speech more impressive.　If you (5.   ) athletes' outstanding speeches, you too can become a speaker who is attractive to your audience.

Activity Plus

You found a victory speech by the tennis player Roger Federer on the Internet.　You are listening to it.

Roger's speech after his final match against Marin Cilic (Croatia) in the 2017 Wimbledon Championships

　Marin Cilic is a hero.　(1.   ) on his running second.　He played perfectly in the final, but it was a bad result for him.　I really hope there will be another good result for him in the future.

　I can't believe I was able to win without losing any sets.　There were times when I couldn't believe I could take part in the final.　However, I decided to believe it.　And Marin and I did it!　It was a great time to be able to (2.   ) with Marin here today.　The center court was filled with a lot of spectators and had a great (3.   ). I will be back here again next year.

　My little sons, watching from their seats, don't know what's going on.　They might think this place is a good (4.   ).　My daughters understand this situation a little, but I will have to talk to them about this again.　I'm so grateful to my family for supporting me!　I couldn't have played in such a wonderful match if I hadn't had your great support.　Thank you again very much.

Part 1 教科書 p.54〜p.55   /54

A Write the English words to match the Japanese. 【知識・技能（語彙）】(各2点)

1. .... 图 災害 B1
2. .... 图 台風
3. .... 圃 絶えず B1
4. .... 圃 つい最近, 先ごろ A2
5. .... 图 干ばつ B2
6. .... 图 爆発 B2

B Choose the word whose underlined part's sound is different from the other three.

【知識・技能（発音）】(各2点)

1. ア．climate   イ．disaster   ウ．natural   エ．volcanic
2. ア．constantly   イ．disaster   ウ．researcher   エ．suggest
3. ア．about   イ．around   ウ．drought   エ．seriously

C Complete the following English sentences to match the Japanese.

【知識・技能（表現・文法）】(完答・各3点)

1. ドアが開いたままになっている。鍵が壊れているようだ。

   The door is left open. It (　　　) (　　　) the lock is broken.
2. その事故は濃霧と関係があるように思えた。

   The thick fog seemed to (　　　) (　　　) to do (　　　) the accident.
3. この地域でのリサイクルに急いで取り組む必要がある。

   We need to (　　　) quickly (　　　) recycling in this area.

D Arrange the words in the proper order to match the Japanese.

【知識・技能（表現・文法）】(各4点)

1. この表は，この店において過去1年でいくつのシャツが売れたかを示している。

   This table shows (at / been / have / how / many / shirts / sold) this store over the past year.

   ----
2. 確かに彼は話すのが下手かもしれませんが，温かい心を持っています。

   It (be / he / is / may / poor / that / true) at talking, but he has a warm heart.

   ----
3. 皆さん，今こそ世界平和に向けて取り組む時です。

   Everyone, (is / now / the time / to / toward / work) world peace.

E Fill in each blank with a suitable word from the passage. 【表現力・判断力・思考力（内容）】(各5点)

1. This is a poster you find at an international event about (　　　) prevention.
2. The graph shows the number of natural disasters reported around the world for (　　　) years since 1990.
3. Natural disasters have caused the deaths of people and (　　　) losses.

26

Part 2　教科書 p.56

/54

A Write the English words to match the Japanese. 【知識・技能（語彙）】（各2点）

1. .... 動 起こる，発生する B1
2. .... 形 特定の B2
3. .... 名 地滑り B2
4. .... 名 インフラ
5. .... 名 避難 B2
6. .... 名 財産，資産 B1

B Choose the word whose stressed syllable is different from the other three.

【知識・技能（発音）】（各2点）

1. ア．dam-age　　イ．land-slide　　ウ．oc-cur　　エ．re-gion
2. ア．man-age-ment　イ．prop-er-ty　ウ．re-cent-ly　エ．se-vere-ly
3. ア．A-mer-i-ca　イ．com-mu-ni-ty　ウ．in-for-ma-tion　エ．par-tic-u-lar

C Complete the following English sentences to match the Japanese.

【知識・技能（表現・文法）】（完答・各3点）

1. ニュートンは重力の法則を発見したと信じられている。

Newton is believed (　　　　) (　　　　) (　　　　) the law of gravity.

2. 今日の午後，私は特にすることがありません。

I have nothing (　　　) (　　　　) to do this afternoon.

3. 運動不足は長い目で見ると健康問題という結果につながる可能性がある。

Lack of exercise can (　　　) (　　　　) health problems in the long run.

D Arrange the words in the proper order to match the Japanese.

【知識・技能（表現・文法）】（各4点）

1. 今は曇っているが，数時間もすると空は明るくなりそうだ。

It's cloudy now, but (clear up / is / likely / the sky / to) in a few hours.

2. その国の全輸出量の約半分を鉱石が占めている。

Minerals (about / account / amount / for / half / of / the total) exports from the country.

3. 自分のためにしていることが，自分の周りの人たちを手助けしているかもしれませんよ。

What you do for yourself (be / helping / may / others) around you.

E Fill in each blank with a suitable word from the passage. 【思考力・判断力・表現力（内容）】（各5点）

1. There are (　　　　) types of natural disasters around the world.
2. One in (　　　　) earthquakes with a magnitude of six or higher occurs in Japan.
3. Even though we have developed infrastructure and trained ourselves, natural disasters continue to destroy life and (　　　　).

Part 3　教科書 p.58　　　/54

A　Write the English words to match the Japanese.　【知識・技能（語彙）】（各2点）

1. .... 副 あらかじめ
2. .... 名 緊急事態 A2
3. .... 名 人気, 評判 B2
4. .... 名 最低限, 最小限 B1
5. .... 形 充電可能な
6. .... 名 懐中電灯

B　Choose the word whose stressed syllable is different from the other three.

【知識・技能（発音）】（各2点）

1. ア．a-void　　　イ．charg-er　　　ウ．flash-light　　　エ．haz-ard
2. ア．dig-it-al　　イ．dis-as-ter　　ウ．min-i-mum　　　エ．now-a-days
3. ア．e-mer-gen-cy　イ．prep-a-ra-tion　ウ．re-charge-a-ble　エ．tech-nol-o-gy

C　Complete the following English sentences to match the Japanese.

【知識・技能（表現・文法）】（完答・各3点）

1. 今日は早く家に帰らないと。明日から始まる修学旅行の準備ができていないんだ。

   I have to get home early today.　I haven't (　　　　) (　　　　) the school trip starting tomorrow.

2. 突然風が吹き込み, ろうそくの火が消えた。

   Suddenly the wind blew in, and the candle (　　　　) (　　　　).

3. その国では常に最新の情報に更新しておいたほうがよいですよ。

   In that country, you should (　　　　) yourself (　　　　) the latest information.

D　Arrange the words in the proper order to match the Japanese.【知識・技能（表現・文法）】（各4点）

1. この電気自動車によって, エネルギー費用にかかる多くのお金を節約することができます。

   This electric vehicle will (a / allow / lot / of / save / to / you) money on energy cost.

   ----

2. すみません。会議室の鍵をなくしたかもしれません。

   I'm sorry.　I (have / lost / may / the key / to) the meeting room.

   ----

3. 江戸時代の日本にはリサイクルのシステムがあったと言われている。

   It (is / recycling systems / said / that / there / were) in Japan in the Edo period.

E　Fill in each blank with a suitable word from the passage.【思考力・判断力・表現力（内容）】（各5点）

1. If you learn about the area where you live, you will be able to avoid potential (　　　　) in the future.

2. (　　　　) food can be eaten with little preparation.

3. You can use an emergency radio as a flashlight and a battery (　　　　) for your digital devices.

Part 4 教科書 p.60

/54

A Write the English words to match the Japanese. 【知識・技能（語彙）】(各2点)

1. _____ 形 知って B1
2. _____ 形 身体に障害を持つ
3. _____ 動 苦労する B2
4. _____ 形 適切な A2
5. _____ 名 絵文字
6. _____ 名 イラスト, 挿し絵 B2

B Choose the word whose underlined part's sound is different from the other three.

【知識・技能（発音）】(各2点)

1. ア．comm<u>u</u>nication　イ．str<u>u</u>ggle　ウ．<u>u</u>nderstand　エ．<u>u</u>pdate
2. ア．Engl<u>i</u>sh　イ．Japan<u>e</u>se　ウ．m<u>e</u>dia　エ．r<u>e</u>cently
3. ア．<u>ch</u>allenge　イ．<u>ch</u>ildren　ウ．ea<u>ch</u>　エ．te<u>ch</u>nology

C Complete the following English sentences to match the Japanese.

【知識・技能（表現・文法）】(完答・各3点)

1. 東南アジアのいくつかの地域は，常に深刻な洪水の危険にさらされている。

   Some areas of Southeast Asia are always (　　　　) (　　　　) of severe floods.

2. 昨夜は本当に寒かったのです。実は雪もたくさん降りました。

   It was really cold last night. (　　　　) (　　　　), it snowed a lot.

3. 本当に準備できているの？　もし試験に受からなければどうするの？

   Are you sure you're prepared? (　　　　) (　　　　) you don't pass the exam?

D Arrange the words in the proper order to match the Japanese.

【知識・技能（表現・文法）】(各4点)

1. 彼らは自分たちの周りで何が起こっているのかもっと気づく必要がある。

   They need to (aware / be / happening / is / more / of / what) around them.

   _____

2. その画家は，1万点以上の作品を生み出したと言われている。

   The painter (have / is / more / produced / said / than / to) 10,000 works.

   _____

3. ウイルスから自分自身や他人を守るのは私たち全員にかかっている。

   It (all / is / of / to / to / up / us) protect ourselves and others from the virus.

   _____

E Fill in each blank with a suitable word from the passage. 【思考力・判断力・表現力（内容）】(各5点)

1. Some (　　　　) from foreign countries cannot understand Japanese.
2. Disaster information which is available in (　　　　) languages can help everyone in a disaster.
3. Thanks to recent ideas and (　　　　), our chances to survive disasters have been improved.

Activity Plus 教科書 p.64〜p.65

/54

A Write the English words to match the Japanese. 【知識・技能（語彙）】（各2点）

1. .... 图 物資, 資源 B1
2. .... 動 避難する B2
3. .... 图 体育館
4. .... 動 …に耐える
5. .... 動 …を補強する B2
6. .... 動 …をふさぐ

B Choose the word whose underlined part's sound is different from the other three.

【知識・技能（発音）】（各2点）

1. ア．reinforce　　イ．great　　ウ．resource　　エ．teacher
2. ア．cardboard　　イ．case　　ウ．evacuate　　エ．face
3. ア．diagonally　　イ．gymnasium　　ウ．item　　エ．night

C Complete the following English sentences to match the Japanese.

【知識・技能（表現・文法）】（完答・各3点）

1. 子供たちは火災の場合に何をすべきか教えられた。

   The children were taught what to do (　　　) (　　　) (　　　) fire.

2. あなたが直面しているその問題について考えてみましょう。

   Let's consider the problem you (　　　) (　　　) (　　　).

3. この戸棚は50キログラムの重さに耐えられるはずだ。

   This shelf should (　　　) the (　　　) of fifty kilograms.

D Arrange the words in the proper order to match the Japanese.

【知識・技能（表現・文法）】（各4点）

1. 役立つかもしれない情報をお持ちならば, 私に知らせてください。

   If you have (be / helpful / information / might / that), let me know.

   ----

2. 外国からの方のために, わかりやすい言葉に変える必要があるかもしれませんね。

   You (change / into / it / may / need / plain / to) words for people from abroad.

   ----

3. 夜にたくさん睡眠をとれば, 生活の中で健康を維持することができます。

   Getting lots of sleep at night can (healthy / help / stay / you) in your life.

E Fill in each blank with a suitable word from the passage. 【思考力・判断力・表現力（内容）】（各5点）

1. The teacher wants the students to think about what items they can create with limited (　　　) in case of a disaster.

2. Koji thinks the cardboard bed can help you stay (　　　) during the night.

3. In order to (　　　) the bed, you can put the pieces of cardboard diagonally into each box.

総合問題

Read the following passage and answer the questions below.

　Recent ideas and technologies allow us to prepare for disasters.　For example, (A)you may (　　　　) (　　　　) about hazard maps.　They tell you the nearest evacuation sites in the areas where disasters are likely to occur.　Learning about the area where you live beforehand, or even after a disaster has happened, will help you avoid potential risks in the future.

　Emergency food is also gaining popularity.　Nowadays, you can buy a variety of foods, (　1　) easy-to-make rice, pre-packaged curry and canned bread.　They can (B)(be / eaten / little / preparation / with) and stored for a couple of years.　It is said that you should store a minimum of a three-day supply of food.　Of course, you can eat the food as part of your daily meals before the food's best-before date.

　(　2　), you need to think about what to do if the power goes out.　An emergency radio can keep you updated with disaster information.　Some radios are rechargeable with solar panels or hand cranks.　You can use such a radio not only as an emergency flashlight but also as a battery charger for your digital devices.　Having such a power source will make a big difference.

1. 下線部(A)が「あなたはハザードマップについて聞いたことがあるかもしれません」という意味に
   なるように，空所に適切な語を補いなさい。　　　　　　　　　　【知識・技能（文法）】（完答・4点）

   ---------------------------　---------------------------

2. 空所(1), (2)に入る適切な語句を選びなさい。　　　　　　【知識・技能（語彙・表現）】（各5点）

   (1)　ア．as such　　　イ．as well　　　ウ．such as　　　エ．well as

   (2)　ア．First　　　イ．For example　　　ウ．In addition　　　エ．In conclusion

3. 下線部(B)の（　　　）内の語を適切に並べかえなさい。　　　【知識・技能（文法）】（5点）

   ----

4. 本文の内容に合っているものをすべて選びなさい。　【思考力・判断力・表現力（内容）】（完答・10点）

   ア．Thanks to recent ideas and technologies, we can prepare for disasters.

   イ．It is not a good idea to use hazard maps after a disaster has happened.

   ウ．Emergency food is becoming more and more popular these days.

   エ．Food companies advise you not to eat emergency food as part of your daily
   　　meals.

   オ．If you want to use an emergency radio as a battery charger, you should
   　　prepare a different one.

5. 次の問いの答えになるよう，空所に適切な語を補いなさい。【思考力・判断力・表現力（内容）】（完答・各8点）

   (1)　How can we know the nearest evacuation sites in the areas where disasters may
   　　occur?
   　　―― We can know them by using (　　　　) (　　　　).

   (2)　In what situation can an emergency radio be useful?
   　　―― It can be useful if the power (　　　　) (　　　　).

ディクテーション

Listen to the English and write down what you hear.

Part 1

You join an international event about disaster (1.　　　). You find a poster.

There Are More Disasters These Days!

We often hear sad news about heavy rains, typhoons and earthquakes. They are (2.　　　) happening all over the world. People are suffering. Their houses are destroyed. They have (3.　　　) to go. "They" may be "you" tomorrow.

The graph shows how many natural disasters have been reported around the world since 1990. It may be true that past disasters are underreported. However, it seems that the number has increased recently. Some researchers (4.　　　) that climate change has something to do with this increase.

Typical examples of natural disasters include floods, droughts, storms, volcanic eruptions and earthquakes. They have caused the deaths of millions of people as well as huge economic (5.　　　). What can we do to deal with these disasters? Now is the time to act seriously on this global issue.

Part 2

More and more natural disasters seem to be happening around the world. Are you well prepared to reduce your own risk from future disasters?

1　Different regions in the world have unique types of natural disasters. Africa tends to suffer from droughts. In Latin America, earthquakes and tsunamis (1.　　　) frequently. Asia is likely to suffer (2.　　　) from floods and storms.

2　Japan is known to have suffered from natural disasters frequently and severely. Earthquakes and typhoons in (3.　　　) have affected our lives. Earthquakes in Japan account for about 20 percent of the world's occurrences with a magnitude of six or higher. Typhoons bring strong winds and heavy rains, resulting in flooding and landslides. Climate change may be increasing the risk of disasters.

3　Traditional approaches to disaster prevention and risk (4.　　　) may not be enough. We have developed infrastructure such as roads, buildings and dams. We have also trained ourselves through (5.　　　) drills at school and in communities. Even so, natural disasters still continue to destroy life and (6.　　　). What else can we do to deal with future disasters?

Part 3

4　Recent ideas and technologies allow us to prepare for disasters. For example, you may have heard about (1.　　　) maps. They tell you the nearest evacuation sites in the areas where disasters are likely to occur. Learning about the area where you live beforehand, or even after a disaster has happened, will help you (2.　　　) potential risks in the future.

5　Emergency food is also gaining popularity. Nowadays, you can buy a variety of foods, such as easy-to-make rice, pre-packaged curry and canned bread. They can be eaten with little preparation and stored for a couple of years. It is said that you should store a (3.　　　) of a three-day supply of food. Of course, you can eat the food as part of your daily meals before the food's best-before date.

6 In addition, you need to think about what to do if the power goes out. An emergency radio can keep you updated with disaster information. Some radios are (4.   ) with solar panels or hand cranks. You can use such a radio not only as an emergency flashlight but also as a battery charger for your (5.   ) devices. Having such a power source will make a big difference.

Part 4

7 We should also be (1.   ) of who is at risk in disasters. You may think of elderly people, little children or physically-challenged people, but you should also think of visitors from foreign countries. Such visitors may have never experienced an earthquake before. Some of them cannot understand Japanese. In fact, visitors are said to have (2.   ) to find proper information in their own languages in past earthquakes in Japan.

8 In order to help foreign people at risk, the use of pictograms and (3.   ) Japanese words has gained attention recently. These communication tools use illustrations and simple expressions so that everybody can understand their messages easily. Some disaster information is also available in foreign languages, such as English, Chinese and Korean, (4.   ) websites, apps and social media. Such information can help everyone in a disaster.

9 Recent ideas and technologies have improved our chances to (5.   ) disasters. However, it is up to each of us to make full use of them. What if a big earthquake happens now? What can you do for yourself, your family and people around you? It is never too early to get prepared.

Activity Plus

A teacher gave students the following task. Koji is now making a (1.   ) presentation about his idea. After that, Airi asks some questions.

Task What items can you create with limited (2.   ) in case of a disaster? Your ideas and knowledge will be important in such a situation. By using the materials below, develop some original items that might be useful if you are faced with a natural disaster.

Koji: My idea is to make a "cardboard bed." In case of a disaster, you may need to (3.   ) from your home and spend several nights in a school gymnasium, for example. You can create a bed with twelve cardboard boxes, twelve pieces of cardboard, and some packaging tape. The bed can help you stay warm during the night. What do you think about my idea?

Airi: That's a great idea, Koji. Can the bed withstand the weight of an adult?

Koji: Thank you for your question. Yes, it can. I forgot to tell you, but you can put the pieces of cardboard (4.   ) into each box to reinforce the bed.

Airi: I see. You then (5.   ) each box with some packaging tape, right?

Koji: Yes. Just putting 12 boxes together creates a bed. You can also cover it with cloth, if you have some.

Part 1 　教科書 p.70〜p.71 　　/54

A Write the English words to match the Japanese. 【知識・技能（語彙）】（各2点）

1. _____ 图 時代, 一時代 B1　　2. _____ 图 始まり, 夜明け B2
3. _____ 動 …を公表する B1　　4. _____ 图 長官 A2
5. _____ 图 作品集　　6. _____ 图 一節 A2

B Choose the word whose stressed syllable is different from the other three.

【知識・技能（発音）】（各2点）

1. ア．an-thol-o-gy　　イ．e-vac-u-ate　　ウ．im-pe-ri-al　　エ．sec-re-tar-y
2. ア．an-nounce　　イ．blos-som　　ウ．men-tion　　エ．pas-sage
3. ア．char-ac-ter　　イ．con-trib-ute　　ウ．gov-ern-ment　　エ．har-mo-ny

C Complete the following English sentences to match the Japanese.

【知識・技能（表現・文法）】（完答・各3点）

1. 彼はトロフィーを掲げて, 喜びを表した。

   He (　　　　) (　　　　) the trophy and expressed his joy.
2. 球団はそのスター選手について公式発表を行った。

   The baseball team made an (　　　　) (　　　　) about the star player.
3. 彼らは次に何が起こるかを見守っている。

   They are (　　　　) (　　　　) (　　　　) what will happen next.

D Arrange the words in the proper order to match the Japanese.

【知識・技能（表現・文法）】（各4点）

1. ハイブリッド車に続いて開発された電気自動車が市場に導入されている。

   Electric cars, (after / developed / hybrid cars / were / which), have been introduced to the market.

   _____
2. そのシリーズは5冊から構成されるだろう。

   The (be / made / of / series / up / will) 5 books.

   _____
3. あなたが今週末, 東京にいるかどうか私に教えてください。

   Please (be / in / know / let / me / whether / will / you) Tokyo this weekend.

   _____

E Fill in each blank with a suitable word from the passage. 【思考力・判断力・表現力（内容）】（各5点）

1. The (　　　　) (　　　　) (　　　　) has announced the name of the new era in Japan.
2. The *Manyoshu* is an ancient (　　　　) of Japanese poetry.
3. People are thinking about whether Japan will (　　　　) to world peace in this new era.

Part 2　教科書 p.72　／54

A　Write the English words to match the Japanese.　【知識・技能（語彙）】（各2点）

1. _____ 動 …を決定する B1
2. _____ 名 考え，概念 B1
3. _____ 動 …を引用する B2
4. _____ 名 文学（作品）B1
5. _____ 動 …を編集する B2
6. _____ 形 無名の

B　Choose the word whose underlined part's sound is different from the other three.

【知識・技能（発音）】（各2点）

1. ア．cab<u>i</u>net　　イ．cl<u>a</u>ssical　　ウ．est<u>a</u>blish　　エ．r<u>a</u>nge
2. ア．anth<u>o</u>logy　　イ．n<u>o</u>tion　　ウ．opp<u>o</u>nent　　エ．p<u>o</u>et
3. ア．<u>au</u>dience　　イ．<u>au</u>nt　　ウ．<u>au</u>spicious　　エ．<u>au</u>thor

C　Complete the following English sentences to match the Japanese.

【知識・技能（表現・文法）】（完答・各3点）

1. ついに彼女はパリに到着し，そこで彼女は旧友に会った。

   Finally, she reached Paris, (　　　　) she met an old friend of hers.

2. スマートウォッチは300ドルから800ドルと価格に幅がある。

   Smartwatches (　　　　) in price from $300 to $800.

3. 日本の自然美を描写する季語がたくさんある。

   There are lots of seasonal words (　　　　) (　　　　) the natural beauty of Japan.

D　Arrange the words in the proper order to match the Japanese.

【知識・技能（表現・文法）】（各4点）

1. 彼はある有名な詩からの1行をスピーチで引用した。

   He (a famous / a line / from / poem / quoted) in his speech.

   _____

2. その辞書は，ある有名な僧侶によって編纂されたと言われています。

   It (compiled / is / said / that / the dictionary / was) by a famous priest.

   _____

3. その入門コースは，その科目が初めての学生のために設計されている。

   The introductory course is designed (are / for / new / students / to / who) the subject.

   _____

E　Fill in each blank with a suitable word from the passage.【思考力・判断力・表現力（内容）】（各5点）

1. "Reiwa" was taken from the *Manyoshu*, the oldest collection of Japanese (　　　　).
2. Public servants living alone also (　　　　) poems to the *Manyoshu*.
3. Japanese people at that time enjoyed *ume* (　　　　) and made poems about them.

Part 3 　教科書 p.74　　／54

A Write the English words to match the Japanese. 【知識・技能（語彙）】（各2点）

1. _____ 名 皇帝 B1
2. _____ 形 稀な，滅多にない B1
3. _____ 名 現象 B1
4. _____ 形 伝説上の B2
5. _____ 形 勢力のある B2
6. _____ 動 …を中止する B1

B Choose the word whose underlined part's sound is different from the other three.

【知識・技能（発音）】（各2点）

1. ア．auth<u>o</u>r　　イ．l<u>or</u>d　　ウ．n<u>or</u>m　　エ．reinf<u>or</u>ce
2. ア．c<u>o</u>met　　イ．gl<u>o</u>be　　ウ．h<u>o</u>nor　　エ．phen<u>o</u>menon
3. ア．<u>a</u>bandon　　イ．<u>a</u>ncient　　ウ．c<u>a</u>lendar　　エ．p<u>a</u>ssage

C Complete the following English sentences to match the Japanese.

【知識・技能（表現・文法）】（完答・各3点）

1. 私たちは「ASAP」という言葉をよく使いますが，それは「as soon as possible」の略です。

   We often use a word "ASAP," which (　　　　) (　　　　) "as soon as possible."

2. 彼はバスケットボールの伝説的なコーチだった。

   He was a (　　　　) basketball coach.

3. 多くの問題があったため，彼らはその計画を断念しなくてはならなかった。

   They had to (　　　　) the plan due to many problems.

D Arrange the words in the proper order to match the Japanese.

【知識・技能（表現・文法）】（各4点）

1. 正式な茶会に着物で出席するのが標準になっている。

   It (a norm / attend / become / has / to) a formal tea party wearing a *kimono*.

   ----

2. 天皇がその都の名を変えたと言われている。

   It (changed / is / that / the emperor / said) the name of the city.

   ----

3. これは非常に良い本だったので，多くの人が読んだ。

   This (a / book / good / such / that / was) many people read it.

E Fill in each blank with a suitable word from the passage. 【思考力・判断力・表現力（内容）】（各5点）

1. In Western countries, people have different (　　　　) of eras, such as "B.C."

2. In ancient China, Emperor Wu changed the era names when (　　　　) natural phenomena appeared or good things happened.

3. Japan is now the only country where both the (　　　　) calendar and era names are used.

Part 4 教科書 p.76～p.77 /54

A Write the English words to match the Japanese. 【知識・技能（語彙）】（各2点）

1. _____ 動 …を示す B2
2. _____ 形 追悼の
3. _____ 動 …を祈る A1
4. _____ 名 慰安 B1
5. _____ 動 …を解釈する B2
6. _____ 動 …を目撃する B1

B Choose the word whose underlined part's sound is different from the other three.

【知識・技能（発音）】（各2点）

1. ア. comf<u>or</u>t   イ. emper<u>or</u>   ウ. minist<u>er</u>   エ. s<u>or</u>t
2. ア. <u>i</u>nterpret   イ. pr<u>i</u>me   ウ. s<u>i</u>gnify   エ. w<u>i</u>tness
3. ア. aw<u>a</u>re   イ. er<u>a</u>   ウ. r<u>a</u>re   エ. sh<u>a</u>re

C Complete the following English sentences to match the Japanese.

【知識・技能（表現・文法）】（完答・各3点）

1. 花言葉では，赤いバラは愛，美，そして情熱を表す。

   In the language of flowers, a red rose (   ) love, beauty and passion.
2. 人は流れ星を幸運のしるしと解釈する。

   People (   ) a shooting star (   ) a lucky sign.
3. 令和時代は私たちの日常生活において多くの変化を目撃してきた。

   The Reiwa era (   ) (   ) a lot of changes in our daily lives.

D Arrange the words in the proper order to match the Japanese.

【知識・技能（表現・文法）】（各4点）

1. 善良な隣人として，私たちはお互い平和に，共に生活すべきだ。

   (in / live / peace / should / together / we) with one another as good neighbors.

   _____
2. 新しい時代が幸せに満ちているという希望をすべての人々が持っている。

   All people have a hope (be / era / full / happiness / new / of / that / the / will).

   _____
3. 私たちはその記憶を次の世代に伝える必要がある。

   We need (down / hand / the memory / to / to) the next generation.

   _____

E Fill in each blank with a suitable word from the passage. 【思考力・判断力・表現力（内容）】（各5点）

1. Japanese people remember Heisei as a (   ) period because there were no wars in Japan.
2. People in Japan hold wishes for world (   ).
3. Most of the events might not be recorded in history books, but they surely remain in our deep (   ).

Activity Plus

教科書 p.80〜p.81

/54

A Write the English words to match the Japanese.　【知識・技能（語彙）】（各2点）

1. _____ 動 …を翻訳する B1
2. _____ 名 名詞 A2
3. _____ 名 動詞 A2
4. _____ 名 形容詞 A2
5. _____ 名 柿
6. _____ 動 (鐘が)鳴る

B Choose the word whose stressed syllable is different from the other three.

【知識・技能（発音）】（各2点）

1. ア．com-pre-hend　　イ．dis-cus-sion　　ウ．per-sim-mon　　エ．trans-la-tion
2. ア．ex-press　　イ．gram-mar　　ウ．name-less　　エ．work-sheet
3. ア．ad-jec-tive　　イ．beau-ti-ful　　ウ．cel-e-brate　　エ．de-ter-mine

C Complete the following English sentences to match the Japanese.

【知識・技能（表現・文法）】（完答・各3点）

1. 何もしないより，何かすることが大切である。

   It is more important to do something (　　　　) (　　　　) nothing.
2. 彼はそのベストセラーの本をイタリア語に訳した。

   He (　　　　) the best-selling book (　　　　) Italian.
3. 彼らはその研究の情報をまとめているところだ。

   They are (　　　　) (　　　　) information on the research.

D Arrange the words in the proper order to match the Japanese.

【知識・技能（表現・文法）】（各4点）

1. 私の父は毎日，コーヒーを1杯飲むことから始める。

   My father (a / coffee / cup / every day / of / starts / with).

   ----
2. 失敗のことは考えないようにするほうがいい。

   You (about / failure / not / should / think / to / try / your).

   ----
3. どうしたら，そのケーキをもっとおいしくすることができるのだろうか。

   How (can / delicious / make / more / the cake / we)?

E Fill in each blank with a suitable word from the passage.

【思考力・判断力・表現力（内容）】（各5点）

1. When you write a *haiku* in English, you don't worry about (　　　　) too much.
2. Satoshi made his translation as clear and easy to comprehend (　　　　) (　　　　).
3. Kazuki said that we should make Satoshi's translation simpler and make it sound more (　　　　) *haiku*.

総合問題

/44

Read the following passage and answer the questions below.

Recent era names in Japan (A)signify a common feeling shared (1) Japanese people. For example, they remember Heisei (2) a peaceful period. There were no wars in Japan in the Heisei era. The Heisei Emperor often went to World War II memorial sites and (B)pray that the spirits of the war dead would rest in peace. (C)This gave Japanese people deep comfort.

On the day when the era name Reiwa was announced, the Prime Minister expressed (D)his hope that the new era would lead to a bright future. He interpreted Reiwa (E)(a / as / beautiful / hearts / people's / time / when) and minds would create a new culture. People in Japan hold wishes (3) world peace. One woman said, "I hope that all children can grow strong in peace in the new era."

(F)Many than 200 era names have been used in Japan, and each era witnessed both good and sad events. Most of those events might not (G)record in history books, but they (H)sure remain in our deep memories. What memory in the new era will be handed down (4) future generations?

1. 下線部(A), (B), (F), (G), (H)の語を適切な形に変えなさい。　【知識・技能（文法）】（各4点）

   (A) ....　(B) ....　(F) ....

   (G) ....　(H) ....

2. 空所(1), (2), (3), (4)に入る適切な語を語群から選んで書きなさい。【知識・技能（語彙・表現）】（各2点）

   (1)(　　　　　)　(2)(　　　　　)　(3)(　　　　　)　(4)(　　　　　)

   〔 as, at, by, for, in, of, to 〕

3. 下線部(C) This が指す内容を日本語で答えなさい。　【思考力・判断力・表現力（内容）】（6点）

   ....

4. 下線部(D) his hope はどんな希望か，日本語で説明しなさい。　【思考力・判断力・表現力（内容）】（6点）

   ....

5. 下線部(E)の (　　　) 内の語を適切に並べかえなさい。　【知識・技能（文法）】（4点）

   ....

ディクテーション

Listen to the English and write down what you hear.

Part 1

As a group project, you are studying the system of the (1.　　　　) era name in Japan. On the Internet, you found a news clip about "Reiwa" and some posts about how people abroad saw the dawn of the new era.

Good afternoon. The name of the new era in Japan has just been (2.　　　　). The name of the new era that follows Heisei will be "Reiwa"! The Chief Cabinet Secretary is now holding up a white card with the new name written in two characters in black ink. "Reiwa" comes from characters used in an (3.　　　　) to some poems in the *Manyoshu*, an ancient anthology of Japanese poetry. This introductory passage (4.　　　　) soft winds and *ume* blossoms in spring.

Victor　What does the new name "Reiwa" mean?

Hiroshi　"Reiwa" is made up of two characters, "rei" and "wa." "Rei" can mean "beautiful" or "good." "Wa" can mean "harmony." The Japanese government made an (5.　　　　) announcement about the English meaning of "Reiwa." It is "the era of beautiful harmony."

Wei　Will Japan choose a beautiful harmony of peace in the new era of "Reiwa"?

Agatha　People around the world are now waiting to see whether Japan will contribute to world peace in this new era.

Part 2

How has the era name in Japan been (1.　　　　)? What meaning does it have to Japanese people?

[1]　The first imperial era in Japan dates back to Taika in 645. The notion of imperial era naming was (2.　　　　) in 701, when the Taiho era began. The names were quoted from classical Chinese literature. Reiwa, on the other hand, was taken from the *Manyoshu*, the oldest collection of Japanese poetry.

[2]　It is said that the *Manyoshu* was (3.　　　　) mainly during the Nara Period, and it contains about 4,500 poems. The (4.　　　　) ranged from celebrated poets to nameless farmers. Public servants living alone far away from their families also contributed. When they made poems, they were able to forget their everyday work for a while and think of their loved ones at home.

[3]　The name Reiwa comes from a line in an introductory passage in the *Manyoshu* which says, "It is now (5.　　　　) early spring; the weather is fine, and the wind is soft." This line describes a party for viewing *ume* blossoms under a sunny spring sky. *Ume* blossoms came from China, and they were new to the Japanese at that time. They enjoyed *ume* blossoms and made poems about them.

Part 3

[4]　When we look around the world, we see different notions of eras. In Western countries, the birth of Jesus Christ became the (1.　　　　) in the Gregorian calendar. In this calendar, "B.C." means "Before Christ" and "A.D." means "Anno Domini," which stands for "in the year of the (2.　　　　)" in Latin.

[5]　In ancient China, Emperor Wu started to name eras in 114 B.C. He changed the era names when rare natural (3.　　　　) appeared or good things happened. For example, it is said that he changed the era name after he saw a comet in the sky and after he hunted a white kylin, a legendary animal in ancient China.

[6]　China was such a large and (4.　　　　) country that neighboring countries

followed the Chinese custom of naming eras. In Japan, for example, Emperor Ichijo changed the era to Eiso in 989, due to the close approach of Halley's Comet. In 1912, China (5.   ) the system of era names and has never used it since. Japan is now the only country where both the Gregorian calendar and era names are used.

Part 4

[7] Recent era names in Japan have (1.   ) a common feeling shared by Japanese people. For example, they remember Heisei as a peaceful period. There were no wars in Japan in the Heisei era. The Heisei Emperor often went to World War II (2.   ) sites and prayed that the spirits of the war dead would rest in peace. This gave Japanese people deep (3.   ).

[8] On the day when the era name Reiwa was announced, the (4.   ) Minister expressed his hope that the new era would lead to a bright future. He (5.   ) Reiwa as a time when people's beautiful hearts and minds would create a new culture. People in Japan hold wishes for world peace. One woman said, "I hope that all children can grow strong in peace in the new era."

[9] More than 200 era names have been used in Japan, and each era witnessed both good and sad events. Most of those events might not be (6.   ) in history books, but they surely remain in our deep memories. What memory in the new era will be handed down to future generations?

Activity Plus

In English class, your teacher gave a (1.   ) to your group. You are listening to a group discussing a student's translation of a *haiku*.

Task (2.   ) the *haiku* below into English.

Tips
- Translate it in three lines.
- Start each line with a small letter.
- You don't need a period at the end.
- Use short and simple words.
- Try not to use "I" or "you."
- Use nouns, rather than (3.   ) or adjectives. If you use verbs, use them in the present tense.
- Don't worry about grammar too much.

Translation : When you eat a (4.   ), you can hear a bell toll at Horyuji. (Satoshi)

Satoshi: I made my translation as clear and easy to (5.   ) as possible. What do you think of it, Kazuki?

Kazuki: You did a good job, but I think this is too long for a translation of a *haiku*. Also, we should try not to use "you." Can't we make it simpler and make it sound more like *haiku*?

Emily: I agree with Kazuki. In English *haiku*, we don't have to start with a (6.   ) letter. We should make it in three lines. I think the first line should be something like "eat a persimmon."

Satoshi: Very good, Emily! Then, the second line can be "and a bell will toll." The final line can be "at Horyuji." Let's put the lines together!

    eat a persimmon
    and a bell will toll
    at Horyuji

Part 1 　教科書 p.86〜p.87　　　/54

A　Write the English words to match the Japanese.　【知識・技能（語彙）】（各2点）

1. .... 图 飢え，飢餓 B1　　2. .... 副 毎年 B1
3. .... 動 …を分配する B1　　4. .... 動 …を消費する B1
5. .... 動 …を暗示する B2　　6. .... 副 平等に B1

B　Choose the word whose underlined part's sound is different from the other three.

【知識・技能（発音）】（各2点）

1. ア．distrib<u>u</u>te　　イ．h<u>u</u>man　　ウ．h<u>u</u>nger　　エ．un<u>u</u>sed
2. ア．annual<u>ly</u>　　イ．equal<u>ly</u>　　ウ．even<u>ly</u>　　エ．imp<u>ly</u>
3. ア．<u>d</u>etermine　　イ．me<u>t</u>ric　　ウ．re<u>d</u>uction　　エ．<u>r</u>equire

C　Complete the following English sentences to match the Japanese.

【知識・技能（表現・文法）】（各3点）

1. 昨日は雨が降っていた。それにもかかわらず，彼女は外出した。

   It was rainy yesterday. (　　　　　), she went out.

2. 彼はハンサムです。その上，サッカーも上手です。

   He is handsome, and (　　　　　), he is good at soccer.

3. 彼らはとても仲がいい。実は来月結婚するらしい。

   They are very close. In (　　　　　), they are going to marry next month.

D　Arrange the words in the proper order to match the Japanese.

【知識・技能（表現・文法）】（各4点）

1. 先生は生徒にプリントを配布します。

   The teacher (distributes / handouts / the students / to).

   ----

2. 私はお母さんがお医者さんの友達がいます。

   I have (a doctor / a friend / is / mother / whose).

   ----

3. 卒業生の4分の1が就職します。

   (fourth / gets / jobs / of / one / the graduates).

E　Fill in each blank with a suitable word from the passage.

【思考力・判断力・表現力（内容）】（各5点）

1. The bill (　　　　) to $100. You can pay it in cash.
2. More than 820 million people in the world are suffering (　　　　) hunger.
3. The truth is (　　　　) one third of the food for human consumption is lost or wasted.

42

Part 2

教科書 p.88～p.89

/54

A　Write the English words to match the Japanese. 　　　　　　　【知識・技能（語彙）】（各2点）

1. _____　名 貯蔵，保管 B1　　　　2. _____　名 設備 B1
3. _____　動 …を輸送する B2　　　4. _____　名 冷蔵，冷凍
5. _____　動 …を捨てる　　　　　　6. _____　形 食べ残しの

B　Choose the word whose stressed syllable is different from the other three.

【知識・技能（発音）】（各2点）

1. ア．dis-card　　　イ．im-ply　　　ウ．stor-age　　　エ．trans-port (v.)
2. ア．an-thol-o-gy　イ．ap-pro-pri-ate　ウ．nev-er-the-less　エ．phe-nom-e-non
3. ア．an-nu-al　　　イ．des-ig-nate　　ウ．fur-ther-more　エ．more-o-ver

C　Complete the following English sentences to match the Japanese.

【知識・技能（表現・文法）】（完答・各3点）

1. 彼は映画を見るのが好きですが，一方，私は本を読む方が好きです。

   He likes to watch movies. (　　　　) the other hand, I like reading books.
2. 彼に以前会ったことがあったのに，名前を忘れてしまった。

   While (　　　) (　　　) him before, I have forgotten his name.
3. 私は英語の勉強もしたいし，さらに，精神面も磨きたい。

   I'd like to study English, and (　　　　), I want to cultivate my mind.

D　Arrange the words in the proper order to match the Japanese.

【知識・技能（表現・文法）】（各4点）

1. 私たちは目標を達成するために努力している。

   We (achieve / an / are / effort / making / to) the goal.

   _____
2. 私の先生は私にやりたいことをするように勧めた。

   My teacher (encouraged / do / I / me / pursue / to / want to / what).

   _____
3. 母は私に必要ないものは捨てなさいと言った。

   My mother told me that I (discard / don't / I / need / should / things).

   _____

E　Fill in each blank with a suitable word from the passage.

【思考力・判断力・表現力（内容）】（各5点）

1. Food may go (　　　　) if it is transported in trucks without refrigeration.
2. Food loss occurs before the food (　　　　) to stores and customers.
3. We need to cut (　　　　) the amount of food loss.

43

Part 3　教科書 p.90　　/54

A Write the English words to match the Japanese.　【知識・技能 (語彙)】(各2点)

1. _____ 動 …を禁止する B2
2. _____ 名 堆肥
3. _____ 名 冷蔵庫 A2
4. _____ 名 家庭, 世帯 B1
5. _____ 形 余分の
6. _____ 動 …を指定する

B Choose the word whose underlined part's sound is different from the other three.

【知識・技能 (発音)】(各2点)

1. ア. di<u>s</u>count　　イ. equipment　　ウ. prohibit　　エ. <u>s</u>idewalk
2. ア. de<u>s</u>ignate　　イ. ex<u>c</u>ess　　ウ. re<u>c</u>ipe　　エ. re<u>t</u>ailer
3. ア. di<u>s</u>card　　イ. f<u>ur</u>thermore　　ウ. occ<u>ur</u>　　エ. s<u>ur</u>plus

C Complete the following English sentences to match the Japanese.

【知識・技能 (表現・文法)】(完答・各3点)

1. あなたが好きな人は誰でも招待していいですよ。

You can invite (　　　　) you like.

2. 私の学校は，災害時の避難所に指定されている。

My school has been (　　　　) (　　　　) an evacuation center in the event of a disaster.

3. 私は3時間ずっとこの本を読んでいます。

I have (　　　　) (　　　　) this book for three hours.

D Arrange the words in the proper order to match the Japanese.

【知識・技能 (表現・文法)】(各4点)

1. 生徒は授業中に携帯電話を使うことは禁止されている。

Students (are / from / mobile phones / prohibited / using) in class.

2. 法律でシートベルトを着用することが求められている。

By law, (are / required / seat belts / to / we / wear).

3. 彼はその本を読み終えたので，図書館に返却した。

(having / he / it / read / returned / the book,) to the library.

E Fill in each blank with a suitable word from the passage.

【思考力・判断力・表現力 (内容)】(各5点)

1. Whoever can take the food in the community fridge (　　　　) free.
2. The movement of setting (　　　　) community refrigerators has been spreading.
3. "World Food Day" was (　　　　) by the United Nations.

Part 4 教科書 p.92

/54

A Write the English words to match the Japanese. 【知識・技能（語彙）】（各2点）

1. _____ 動 …に取り組む B2   2. _____ 名 小売業者 B2

3. _____ 名 値引き B1   4. _____ 形 売れ残りの

5. _____ 動 …を買う B2   6. _____ 動 だめになる B1

B Choose the word whose stressed syllable is different from the other three.

【知識・技能（発音）】（各2点）

1. ア．com-post   イ．pur-chase   ウ．sur-plus   エ．un-sold

2. ア．dis-count   イ．ex-cess   ウ．near-by   エ．un-used

3. ア．left-over   イ．re-quire   ウ．side-walk   エ．tack-le

C Complete the following English sentences to match the Japanese.

【知識・技能（表現・文法）】（完答・各3点）

1. このプログラムは生徒の英語力向上に役立ちます。

   This program (　　　　) (　　　　) students' English ability.

2. 生徒たちは歌詞を曲に合わせるのに苦労した。

   It was hard for the students to (　　　　) the words (　　　　) the music.

3. 私たちの努力は報われませんでした。

   Our effort didn't (　　　　) (　　　　).

D Arrange the words in the proper order to match the Japanese.

【知識・技能（表現・文法）】（各4点）

1. 問題を解決するもう1つの方法は，お金を節約することです。

   (another / is / solve / the problem / to / way) to save money.

   _____

2. あなたはそれを共有できる人を見つけるために，このアプリを使うことができる。

   You can use (it / someone / this app / to find / to share / with).

   _____

3. 最近さまざまなフードシェアリングアプリが開発されている。

   Recently, (apps / been / developed / food-sharing / have / various).

   _____

E Fill in each blank with a suitable word from the passage.

【思考力・判断力・表現力（内容）】（各5点）

1. We will have a world free (　　　　) hunger when our efforts bear fruit.

2. Shoppers use the app to buy unsold foods cheaply and pick them (　　　　) at the supermarket later.

3. Some restaurants may have a surplus of food (　　　　) will spoil soon.

Activity Plus 　教科書 p.96〜p.97

 /54

A　Write the English words to match the Japanese.　【知識・技能（語彙）】（各 2 点）

1. .... 图 アンケート B1　　2. .... 動 答える B1
3. .... 形 オンラインの A2　　4. .... 形 補助の A2
5. .... 图 選択肢 B1　　6. .... 图 漬け物 B2

B　Choose the word whose stressed syllable is different from the other three.

【知識・技能（発音）】（各 2 点）

1. ア．ac-tive　　　　イ．ad-vance　　　　ウ．re-spond　　　　エ．un-sold
2. ア．con-sume　　　イ．house-hold　　　ウ．op-tion　　　　エ．pur-chase
3. ア．in-for-ma-tion　イ．pre-sen-ta-tion　ウ．trans-por-ta-tion エ．un-hap-pi-ness

C　Complete the following English sentences to match the Japanese.

【知識・技能（表現・文法）】（各 3 点）

1. 私の父は賞味期限を気にしすぎる。

   My father (　　　　) too much attention to best-before dates.
2. 残り物を捨てる代わりに，冷蔵庫に保存しましょう。

   Let's store leftovers in the fridge (　　　　) of throwing them away.
3. その会社はその野菜で漬け物を作っています。

   That company makes pickles (　　　　) that vegetable.

D　Arrange the words in the proper order to match the Japanese.

【知識・技能（表現・文法）】（各 4 点）

1. 私はあなたにこのアンケートに記入してもらいたい。

   I (fill / like / out / this questionnaire / to / would / you).

   ....

2. それは冷蔵庫に何が残っているのかを忘れないようにする。

   It (forget / helps / not / the leftovers / to / you) in the refrigerator.

   ....

3. あなたは，フードロスをなくすために家で何かしていることはありますか。

   Do you (do / food loss / reduce / something / to) in your home?

   ....

E　Fill in each blank with a suitable word from the passage.

【思考力・判断力・表現力（内容）】（各 5 点）

1. You have to respond (　　　　) an online questionnaire.
2. Thank you (　　　　) advance for your help.
3. This is a slide explaining the results (　　　　) the questionnaire.

総合問題

/50

Read the following passage and answer the questions below.

France was (A)(a law / country / food waste / the first / to make / to reduce).　Since 2016, large supermarkets have been prohibited (1) throwing away food.　(2), they have been required to donate it or turn it into compost or animal feed.　France has become a leader in food waste reduction and has inspired other countries.

In the Spanish town of Galdakao, a community refrigerator was placed on a sidewalk in 2015.　People from nearby restaurants and households put their excess food and leftovers into the fridge, and (3) wants them can take them for free.　The movement of setting up community refrigerators has been spreading to many other countries, including the U.K., Belgium, Argentina and Israel.

October 16 is "World Food Day," which was established by the United Nations.　In Japan, the entire month of October has been designated as "World Food Day Month."　During this period, various food events are held all over Japan.　(4), in an event in 2019, participants (B)(recipes / to post / using / unused food / were asked) on social media.　Sponsors of the event donated 120 yen per post to a charity that supported school meals in Africa.

1. 空所(1), (2), (3), (4)に入る適切な語を選びなさい。　【知識・技能（語彙・表現）】（各4点）

   (1)　ア. at　　　　　　イ. from　　　　　ウ. of　　　　　　エ. on
   (2)　ア. By the way　イ. Finally　　　　ウ. However　　　エ. Instead
   (3)　ア. whatever　　イ. whenever　　　ウ. whichever　　エ. whoever
   (4)　ア. After all　　イ. For example　　ウ. In addition　エ. Therefore

2. 下線部(A), (B)の（　　）内の語句を適切に並べかえなさい。　【知識・技能（文法）】（各5点）

   (A) --
   (B) --

3. 本文の内容に合っているものをすべて選びなさい。　【思考力・判断力・表現力（内容）】（完答・8点）

   ア. Community refrigerators have been set up not only in European countries but also in other countries.

   イ. Large supermarkets have been throwing away food since 2016 in France.

   ウ. Community refrigerators were first placed on sidewalks in France.

   エ. Participants in a 2019 event in Japan donated 120 yen to a charity that supported school meals in Africa.

   オ. The entire month of October has been designated as "World Food Day Month" in Japan.

4. 次の問いの答えになるよう，空所に適切な語を補いなさい。【思考力・判断力・表現力（内容）】（完答・各8点）

   (1) What do large supermarkets in France do to reduce food waste?
   　　——They (　　　　　) food or turn it into (　　　　　) or animal feed.

   (2) How much does it cost if people in Spain take food from a community refrigerator?
   　　——They can take food (　　　　　)(　　　　　).

ディクテーション

Listen to the English and write down what you hear.

Part 1

You want to gather information about food loss and waste. You found a Q&A site.
Is it true that there is enough food to feed all the people on the earth?　　Lilly

Answer
Takehiko Ogawa, a social studies teacher at a high school in Japan since 2001

　It's true that we can feed everyone on the earth. For example, about 2.6 billion metric tons of cereals are produced (1.　　　) all over the world. If they were (2.　　　) evenly to all of the people around the world, each person could have over 330 kilograms of cereals to eat in a year. That is more than double the amount that a Japanese (3.　　　) in a year.

　Nevertheless, it is also true that more than 820 million people, or one in nine people in the world, are suffering from (4.　　　). This implies that food is not equally available to everyone. In fact, about half the cereals produced worldwide are consumed in developed countries, whose population is less than 20% of the world population.

　Moreover, the (5.　　　) is that about one third of the food produced for human consumption is lost or wasted every year. This amounts to about 1.3 billion (6.　　　) tons. If we save one fourth of the lost or wasted food, we will save enough food for all the hungry people in the world.

Part 2

The world population is estimated to reach 9.7 billion in 2050, and global food problems are expected to become even more serious.

1　Too much food produced for human beings is lost or wasted in the food supply chain. Food loss occurs early in the chain——before the food even gets to stores and consumers. For example, in developing countries, farmers lose a large part of their (1.　　　) because they don't have appropriate storage equipment. Food is often eaten by (2.　　　) and small creatures. Furthermore, food is sometimes lost during transportation. For instance, food may go bad if it is (3.　　　) in trucks without refrigeration.

2　On the other hand, food waste occurs at the end of the chain——in stores, restaurants and houses. Food that is past its best-before date is (4.　　　) at grocery stores, and uneaten food is thrown away at restaurants. In our home, (5.　　　) food goes bad in the fridge and is thrown away.

3　Having recognized the importance of reducing food loss and waste, the United Nations is encouraging people to take action. As one of the targets of SDGs, we need to reduce food waste by half and cut down the amount of food loss by 2030. Governments, organizations and individuals around the world have begun to make efforts to achieve this target.

Part 3

4　France was the first country to make a law to reduce food waste. Since 2016, large supermarkets have been (1.　　　) from throwing away food. Instead, they have been required to donate it or turn it into compost or animal feed. France has become a leader in food waste (2.   ) and has inspired other countries.

⑤ In the Spanish town of Galdakao, a community refrigerator was placed on a sidewalk in 2015. People from (3.   ) restaurants and households put their excess food and leftovers into the fridge, and whoever wants them can take them for free. The movement of setting up community refrigerators has been spreading to many other countries, including the U.K., Belgium, Argentina and Israel.

⑥ October 16 is "World Food Day," which was established by the United Nations. In Japan, the entire month of October has been (4.   ) as "World Food Day Month." During this period, various food events are held all over Japan. For example, in an event in 2019, participants were asked to post recipes using (5.   ) food on social media. Sponsors of the event donated 120 yen per post to a charity that supported school meals in Africa.

Part 4

⑦ Another way to (1.   ) the problem of food loss and waste is to use technology. Recently, various food-sharing apps have been developed and are receiving special attention. These apps help match people who don't want to discard food with people who need it.

⑧ Some apps connect a person to another person. When you have more food than you can eat in your home, you can use these apps to find someone to share it with. Other apps link (2.   ) to shoppers. A supermarket can post discount information about unsold food. Shoppers can (3.   ) this unsold food cheaply with the app and come to the supermarket later to pick it up. There are also some apps that connect stores to charity organizations. When a restaurant has a surplus of food that will (4.   ) soon, it can donate the food. These apps help reduce food loss and waste at every point along the food supply chain.

⑨ Food loss and waste is a global issue. Everyone in the world has to understand the causes of this problem and make an effort to solve it. When these efforts bear fruit, we will finally have a world free of hunger.

Activity Plus

You responded to an online (1.   ) made by your Assistant Language Teacher. After all the students answered, a (2.   ) with a graph was generated.

Introduction

I am studying about food loss and waste in daily life. I would like to ask you to fill out this questionnaire. It only takes about five minutes. The results will be used for my study, and I will give a research presentation at a later date. Thank you in (3.   ) for your help.

Questionnaire about food loss and waste

Q. Are you or your family members doing something to reduce food waste in your home? Please check all the actions that are true for your family, and then check who is/are doing them. (You may choose more than one (4.   ).)

Part 1
教科書 p.102〜p.103

/54

A　Write the English words to match the Japanese.　【知識・技能（語彙）】（各2点）

1. .... 图 対話 B1
2. .... 图 大陸 A2
3. .... 图 探検家 B2
4. .... 图 グランドスラム
5. .... 图 達成，業績
6. .... 图 極 B1

B　Choose the word whose underlined part's sound is different from the other three.

【知識・技能（発音）】（各2点）

1. ア．Antarct<u>i</u>ca　　イ．cl<u>i</u>mb　　　ウ．d<u>i</u>alogue　　エ．h<u>i</u>ghest
2. ア．c<u>o</u>ntinent　　イ．dial<u>o</u>gue　　ウ．expl<u>o</u>rer　　エ．supp<u>o</u>rt
3. ア．<u>a</u>ccomplishment　イ．Al<u>a</u>ska　　ウ．gr<u>a</u>nd　　　エ．m<u>a</u>p

C　Complete the following English sentences to match the Japanese.

【知識・技能（表現・文法）】（完答・各3点）

1. ヴィンソン・マシフは南極大陸に位置している。

　Vinson Massif is located in the (　　　　　) of Antarctica.

2. さやかとジェーンを含めて約20人がパーティーに参加した。

　About twenty people, (　　　　　) Sayaka and Jane, joined the party.

3. 「日本での新しい生活はどうですか。」「これまでのところすべて順調ですよ。」

　"How is your new life in Japan?" —— "Everything is going well (　　　　) (　　　　)."

D　Arrange the words in the proper order to match the Japanese.【知識・技能（表現・文法）】（各4点）

1. ここに手話を教えてくれるよい本がありますよ。

　Here is (a / book / nice / teaches / that / you) sign language.

　---

2. 法隆寺は7世紀に建てられており，世界最古の木造建築物である。

　Horyuji Temple, which was built in the seventh century, is (in / oldest / structure / the / wooden) the world.

　---

3. エドモンド・ヒラリーはエベレストの頂上に世界で初めて到達した人として知られている。

　Edmund Hillary is known to be the (first / in / person / reach / the world / to) the top of Mt. Everest.

E　Fill in the blank with a suitable word from the passage.【思考力・判断力・表現力（内容）】（各5点）

1. This is a map which shows the highest mountain on each (　　　　).

2. The Explorer's Grand Slam is the (　　　　) of climbing the Seven Summits and going to the North and South Poles.

3. A Japanese woman became the youngest person to (　　　　) the achievement in 2017.

Part 2 　教科書 p.106〜p.107

/54

A　Write the English words to match the Japanese.　【知識・技能（語彙）】（各2点）

1. ....　動 努力する B2
2. ....　形 無限の
3. ....　動 …を確認する B2
4. ....　名 心配, 不安 B1
5. ....　形 壮大な B1
6. ....　名 存在 B1

B　Choose the word whose stressed syllable is different from the other three.

【知識・技能（発音）】（各2点）

1. ア．ex-plore　　イ．main-land　　ウ．pas-sion　　エ．trad-ing
2. ア．con-ti-nent　　イ．ex-ist-ence　　ウ．in-fi-nite　　エ．mo-ti-vate
3. ア．anx-i-e-ty　　イ．dif-fi-cul-ty　　ウ．i-den-ti-fy　　エ．mag-nif-i-cent

C　Complete the following English sentences to match the Japanese.

【知識・技能（表現・文法）】（完答・各3点）

1. 祖父は若いころ鉄道会社で勤務していた。

   My grandfather (　　　　) (　　　　) a railway company when he was young.
2. 彼は1年間マレーシアに留学する機会を得た。

   He had an (　　　　) (　　　　) study in Malaysia for a year.
3. 大きな音がしたが，まるで何事も起こらなかったかのように彼女は話し続けた。

   There was a loud noise, but she kept talking (　　　　) (　　　　) nothing had happened.

D　Arrange the words in the proper order to match the Japanese.【知識・技能（表現・文法）】（各4点）

1. そのレポートによると，アメリカ人の約80％が自分をキリスト教徒だと認識している。

   According to the report, about eighty percent (American / as / Christians / identify / of / people / themselves).

2. もう少し早く家を出ていれば日の出が見られたのだが。

   I could (had / have / I / if / left / seen / the sunrise) home a little earlier.

3. このウェブサイトは防災に関する便利な情報を提供している。

   This website (information / provides / useful / with / you) on disaster prevention.

E　Fill in each blank with a suitable word from the passage.【思考力・判断力・表現力（内容）】（各5点）

1. At the age of (　　　　), Marin completed the Explorer's Grand Slam.
2. Climbing mountains with her (　　　　) became a turning point in Marin's life.
3. Marin wanted to explore herself and learn the purpose of her (　　　　).

Part 3 教科書 p.108〜p.109 /54

A Write the English words to match the Japanese. 【知識・技能 (語彙)】(各2点)

1. _____ 名 夢, 大望 A2　　2. _____ 名 援助 B1

3. _____ 動 成功する A2　　4. _____ 形 否定的な A2

5. _____ 名 会社, 商社 B1　　6. _____ 動 …を征服する B1

B Choose the word whose stressed syllable is different from the other three.

【知識・技能 (発音)】(各2点)

1. ア. a-rise　　　　イ. con-quer　　　ウ. re-quest　　　エ. suc-ceed

2. ア. am-bi-tion　　イ. as-sis-tance　　ウ. fi-nan-cial　　エ. neg-a-tive

3. ア. in-for-ma-tion　イ. e-co-nom-ics　ウ. fi-nan-cial-ly　エ. prep-a-ra-tion

C Complete the following English sentences to match the Japanese.

【知識・技能 (表現・文法)】(完答・各3点)

1. 私の弟はもう, 物事の善し悪しの判断ができる歳です。

   My younger brother is now (　　　　) (　　　　) to tell right from wrong.

2. このパズルは私には解くのが難しい。あきらめなければならないと思う。

   This puzzle is hard for me to solve. I think I have to (　　　　) (　　　　).

3. 彼が仕事について不平を言うのをこれまで一切聞いたことがありません。

   Never (　　　　) I (　　　　) him complaining about his job.

D Arrange the words in the proper order to match the Japanese.

【知識・技能 (表現・文法)】(各4点)

1. 東京で一人暮らしをするのにどれくらいお金が必要になるのか知りたい。

   I want to know how much money I need to (live / my / on / own) in Tokyo.

   _____

2. ついに, なんとか一輪車に乗れるようになる日がやってきた。

   Finally, (came / I / managed / the day / when) to ride on my unicycle.

   _____

3. 昨日になって初めて, 私たちは彼が言っていたことが誤りだと気づいた。

   Not until yesterday (did / realize / that / we) what he had said was false.

   _____

E Fill in each blank with a suitable word from the passage.

【思考力・判断力・表現力 (内容)】(各5点)

1. Marin's father said that he wouldn't (　　　　) her financially in her challenge.

2. When she was a high school student, Marin climbed Mt. (　　　　).

3. After she succeeded in climbing Mt. Everest, Marin set her (　　　　) on the Explorer's Grand Slam.

Part 4　教科書 p.110〜p.111　／54

A　Write the English words to match the Japanese.　【知識・技能（語彙）】（各2点）

1. _____ 動 …を成し遂げる B1
2. _____ 動 …を証明する B1
3. _____ 形 人力で動く
4. _____ 動 …を織る
5. _____ 名 模様，柄 B1
6. _____ 名 飛躍 B2

B　Choose the word whose underlined part's sound is different from the other three.

【知識・技能（発音）】（各2点）

1. ア．h<u>o</u>pe　　イ．m<u>o</u>tivation　　ウ．p<u>o</u>le　　エ．pr<u>o</u>ve
2. ア．gr<u>ea</u>t　　イ．l<u>ea</u>p　　ウ．r<u>ea</u>ch　　エ．w<u>ea</u>ve
3. ア．a<u>ch</u>ievement　　イ．<u>ch</u>ildren　　ウ．rea<u>ch</u>　　エ．ya<u>ch</u>t

C　Complete the following English sentences to match the Japanese.

【知識・技能（表現・文法）】（完答・各3点）

1. その家族は，親戚に会うために福岡に向けて出発した。

The family (　　　) (　　　) for Fukuoka to meet their relatives.

2. 勝利に向けて努力することで，その選手たちはチームワークを高めることができるだろう。

Striving toward victory will (　　　) the players (　　　) improve their teamwork.

3. あなたの願いがかなうとよいですね。

I hope you can make your wish (　　　) (　　　).

D　Arrange the words in the proper order to match the Japanese.

【知識・技能（表現・文法）】（各4点）

1. 父は，固い信念がなければ何事も成し遂げることはできないと教えてくれた。

My father taught me (accomplished / be / could / nothing / without) firm faith.

_____

2. たとえ気が進まなくても，彼は外出しなければならないだろう。

He will have to (be / even / go / he / may / out / though) unwilling to.

_____

3. あらゆる小さなことが結び付いて，大きな意味をもたらすだろう。

Every small thing will (a / big / combine / difference / make / to).

_____

E　Fill in each blank with a suitable word from the passage.【思考力・判断力・表現力（内容）】（各5点）

1. Marin's accomplishment proves that there is (　　　) we cannot do if we keep trying.

2. Marin thinks that living is like weaving a (　　　) whose patterns and colors are determined by how we live.

3. Marin thinks that your (　　　) are the strongest things to make your dreams come true.

Activity Plus 教科書 p.116〜p.117 /54

A Write the English words to match the Japanese. 【知識・技能（語彙）】（各2点）

1. .... 形 詳細な B2
2. .... 形 地域の B1
3. .... 動 …を広げる B2
4. .... 图 観点，視点 B2
5. .... 動 参加する B1
6. .... 图 運用力 B1

B Choose the word whose underlined part's sound is different from the other three.

【知識・技能（発音）】（各2点）

1. ア．academic　　イ．action　　ウ．chart　　エ．command
2. ア．definitely　　イ．detailed　　ウ．realize　　エ．regional
3. ア．college　　イ．economics　　ウ．participate　　エ．perspective

C Complete the following English sentences to match the Japanese.

【知識・技能（表現・文法）】（完答・各3点）

1. 私は，昨日起こった事故に関する詳細な記事を見つけた。

   I found some (　　　) articles on the accident which happened yesterday.
2. 私たちが家に着くまでに，太陽は完全に沈んでいるだろう。

   (　　　) the (　　　) we get home, the sun will have completely set.
3. 文法をうまく使える力は，外国語で人々と意思疎通をするのに重要である。

   A good (　　　) (　　　) grammar is important to communicate with people in a foreign language.

D Arrange the words in the proper order to match the Japanese. 【知識・技能（表現・文法）】（各4点）
1. 昨夜，私はテレビを見ながら眠ってしまった。

   Last night I (asleep / fell / TV / watching / while).

2. 私たちが富士山の頂上から見た雄大な景色を私は忘れることができない。

   I can't forget (from / magnificent / saw / the / view / we) the top of Mt. Fuji.

3. 彼は日本の将来について考えるために，経済学の討論に参加することを計画している。

   He is planning to (discussions / economics / in / on / participate / to) think about the future of Japan.

E Fill in each blank with a suitable word from the passage. 【思考力・判断力・表現力（内容）】（各4点）
1. She will improve her (　　　) abilities during high school.
2. Her club's goal is to participate in the (　　　) tournament.
3. She plans to study economics and gain a good (　　　) of several languages to realize her dream.

総合問題

Read the following passage and answer the questions below.

When Marin was 17, she started preparing for climbing Mt. Everest. She told her father about her ambition. However, he said, "I won't support you financially. This is your project and you're old enough (A)(do / figure / on / out / to / to / what) your own." Since she had no assistance, she had to request support from companies while studying and training. Some people told her she would not succeed. (1), a strong will arose in her and defeated such negative words. She thought, "If I give up, I will be a person who never tried anything." Luckily, she received financial support from many firms.

As a first step, Marin climbed Mt. Aconcagua in her last year of high school. In the following year, she climbed Mt. Kilimanjaro, Mont Blanc and Mt. Manaslu. Finally, the day came (2) her dream was realized. In May 2016, at the age of 19, she was standing on Everest above the clouds, above all her difficulties.

Marin's dream kept (B)(grow) as she conquered more mountains. Never (C)(challenging / did / herself / she / stop), even though some people said her challenges were impossible. She set her sights on the Seven Summits and, eventually, on the Explorer's Grand Slam.

1. 下線部(A), (C)の (   ) 内の語を適切に並べかえなさい。 【知識・技能（文法）】（各4点）

   (A) --

   (C) --

2. 空所(1), (2)に入る適切な語を選びなさい。 【知識・技能（語彙・表現）】（各4点）

   (1) ア．Also   イ．Although   ウ．However   エ．Or

   (2) ア．how   イ．if   ウ．when   エ．where

3. 下線部(B) grow を適切な形に変えなさい。 【知識・技能（文法）】（4点）

   (   )

4. 本文の内容に合うものをすべて選びなさい。 【知識・技能（語彙）】（完答・10点）

   ア．At the age of 17, Marin succeeded in climbing Mt. Everest.

   イ．Marin refused to accept her father's offer and began requesting support from companies.

   ウ．Marin didn't want to be a person who never tried anything.

   エ．After she graduated from high school, Marin climbed Mt. Kilimanjaro.

   オ．When she stood on the top of Mt. Everest, Marin completed the Explorer's Grand Slam.

5. 次の問いの答えになるよう，空所に適切な語を補いなさい。【思考力・判断力・表現力（内容）】（完答・各8点）

   (1) What did Marin's father tell her when she told him about her ambition?

       ── He told her that he wouldn't (   ) her (   ).

   (2) How long did it take Marin to climb Mt. Everest after she started preparing for climbing it?

       ── It took her about (   ) years.

ディクテーション

Listen to the English and write down what you hear.

Part 1

Koji and an Assistant Language Teacher are talking about a map of the world.

Koji: What's that?

ALT: Hi, Koji! It's a map that shows the highest mountain on each ($1.$).

Koji: Wow, how interesting! I know you like climbing mountains. Where would you like to go?

ALT: I want to climb Mt. Everest someday. Do you know about the Explorer's Grand Slam? It is the ($2.$) of climbing the highest mountain on each continent, including Mt. Everest, and going to the North and South ($3.$).

Koji: Oh, wow! That must be very hard to do. How many people have done it?

ALT: About 50 people have done it so far! And a female Japanese university student became the youngest person in the world to complete this great ($4.$) in 2017.

Part 2

Marin Minamiya completed a remarkable achievement. What ($1.$) her? What made her reach for her dream?

① "Strive toward your goal with passion. Nothing is stronger than our will. A person's potential is truly ($2.$)," says Marin Minamiya. She completed the Explorer's Grand Slam when she was 20 years old.

② Marin was born in Tokyo on December 20, 1996. Since her father worked for a ($3.$) company, her family moved to various places, including Malaysia, mainland China and Hong Kong. She lived outside Japan from a young age, and it was difficult for her to ($4.$) herself as Japanese. When she was 13 years old in Hong Kong, she got an opportunity to climb some mountains with her classmates. This became a turning point in her life. Each climb taught her something new, and afterward she felt as if she had escaped from all stress and ($5.$).

③ One day, Marin went trekking in Nepal, and she saw Mt. Everest for the first time. Everything about the magnificent mountain was eye-opening for her. The experience inspired her greatly and provided her with courage, faith and power. She said, "I knew that I would come back to the great Everest one day. I wanted to explore myself and learn the purpose of my ($6.$)."

Part 3

④ When Marin was 17, she started preparing for climbing Mt. Everest. She told her father about her ($1.$). However, he said, "I won't support you financially. This is your project and you're old enough to figure out what to do on your own." Since she had no assistance, she had to ($2.$) support from companies while studying and training. Some people told her she would not succeed. However, a strong will arose in her and defeated such (3.   ) words. She thought, "If I give up, I will be a person who never tried anything." Luckily, she received financial support from many (4.   ).

⑤ As a first step, Marin climbed Mt. Aconcagua in her last year of high school. In the following year, she climbed Mt. Kilimanjaro, Mont Blanc and Mt. Manaslu. Finally, the day came when her dream was realized. In May 2016, at the age of 19, she was standing on Everest above the clouds, above all her difficulties.

⑥ Marin's dream kept growing as she (5.   ) more mountains. Never did she stop challenging herself, even though some people said her challenges were impossible. She set her sights on the Seven Summits and, eventually, on the Explorer's Grand Slam.

| Part 4 |

⑦ Marin has (1.   ) the Explorer's Grand Slam, proving that there is nothing we cannot do if we keep trying. "Am I what I want to be?" This question made her set out for the mountains. Climbing mountains and keeping her motivation enabled her to (2.   ) herself and conquer her weaknesses. They taught her that anything could be attained; any summit could be reached, no matter how high it might be.

⑧ Marin is now preparing for her next adventure. She hopes to (3.   ) to various countries with a human-powered yacht and talk about life and the future with children there. Marin says, "To live is to (4.   ) your tapestry with different patterns. The patterns and colors in our tapestries are determined by how we live. We need to ask ourselves what we want to do in order to make our own special tapestries."

⑨ This is Marin's message to us all: "Even though your steps may seem small, they will surely combine to become a great (5.   ) to make your future better. Believe that you are going to make it through everything you are doing. There is nothing as strong as your passions to make your dreams come true."

| Activity Plus |

In class, students are sharing their plans for the future while showing (1.   ) about their goals. You are listening to a student's presentation about her goals and action plans.

Hi! Here are my future goals and the (2.   ) actions I will take to achieve them. During high school, I will improve my academic abilities. I study hard in every class and at home. I'm in the tennis club and our team has a goal of participating in the (3.   ) tournament. All the members of my club practice very hard. During college, I will broaden my perspectives and meet many new people from around the world. By the time I'm 30 years old, I (4.   ) want to work for a trading company. To realize my dream, I plan to study economics and gain a good (5.   ) of several languages. Thank you for listening.

Part 1　教科書 p.122〜p.123

/54

A　Write the English words to match the Japanese.　【知識・技能（語彙）】（各2点）

1. _____ 名 マニュアル B2
2. _____ 形 最新の B1
3. _____ 動 …に充電する B1
4. _____ 名 アダプター
5. _____ 副 正しく A2
6. _____ 形 非認定の B2

B　Choose the word whose underlined part's sound is different from the other three.

【知識・技能（発音）】（各2点）

1. ア．b<u>a</u>ttery　　イ．d<u>a</u>mage　　ウ．m<u>a</u>nual　　エ．r<u>a</u>nge
2. ア．<u>a</u>dapter　　イ．c<u>o</u>ntact　　ウ．pr<u>o</u>perly　　エ．w<u>a</u>tch
3. ア．<u>au</u>thorized　　イ．b<u>ou</u>ght　　ウ．br<u>oa</u>den　　エ．h<u>ou</u>sehold

C　Complete the following English sentences to match the Japanese.

【知識・技能（表現・文法）】（完答・各3点）

1. ルイスさんにおつなぎします。

   I'll (　　　　) you (　　　　) Mr. Lewis.
2. 私の大好きな歌手が今晩テレビ番組に出演します。

   My favorite singer will (　　　　) (　　　　) a TV show tonight.
3. このスマートフォンは特にお年寄り向けにデザインされました。

   This smartphone was designed (　　　　) (　　　　) the elderly.

D　Arrange the words in the proper order to match the Japanese.

【知識・技能（表現・文法）】（各4点）

1. 外出するときは，すべての窓が施錠されているのを確認してください。

   (all / are / locked / make / sure / windows) when you go out.

   ----
2. 子供たちがその公園に着くのに30分かかった。

   It (for / get / the children / 30 minutes / to / to / took) the park.

   ----
3. 屋外でのプリンターの使用は，インクシステムを損傷する可能性があります。

   Using (a printer / damage / may / outdoors / the ink) system.

E　Fill in each blank with a suitable word from the passage.

【思考力・判断力・表現力（内容）】（各5点）

1. Before using a smartwatch, you should read the user (　　　　) to find out how to charge it.
2. When you charge your smartwatch, (　　　　) the watch on the charger.
3. When the watch fully charges, "100%" will be (　　　　) on the watch screen.

Part 2

教科書 p.124～p.125

/54

A Write the English words to match the Japanese. 【知識・技能（語彙）】（各2点）

1. _____ 動 存在する A2
2. _____ 名 革新 B2
3. _____ 名 影響，衝撃 A2
4. _____ 形 効率的な B1
5. _____ 形 初期の，一次の B2
6. _____ 動 …を占める B1

B Choose the word whose underlined part's sound is different from the other three.

【知識・技能（発音）】（各2点）

1. ア．accomplish　　イ．innovation　　ウ．occupy　　エ．technological
2. ア．exist　　イ．hybrid　　ウ．landfill　　エ．mobile
3. ア．energy　　イ．evenly　　ウ．lessen　　エ．primary

C Complete the following English sentences to match the Japanese.

【知識・技能（表現・文法）】（完答・各3点）

1. ストレスは私たちの健康に影響を及ぼす。

   Stress has an (　　　　) (　　　　) our health.

2. 私たちが住む場所を選ぶときには，いくつかの要素が関与する。

   Several factors (　　　　) (　　　　) (　　　　) when we choose a place to live.

3. 数十億ドルがその会社に投資されてきた。

   (　　　　) (　　　　) dollars have been invested in that company.

D Arrange the words in the proper order to match the Japanese.

【知識・技能（表現・文法）】（各4点）

1. あなたのアドバイスがなかったら，私は成功しなかっただろう。

   Without (advice, / have / I / not / succeeded / would / your).

   _____

2. 私たちは次の試合に勝つために，一生懸命練習しています。

   We are practicing very hard (game / in / next / order / the / to / win).

   _____

3. ソーシャルメディアは多くの人に影響を与える手段として使われます。

   Social media are used (a / as / influence / means / to) many people.

   _____

E Fill in each blank with a suitable word from the passage. 【思考力・判断力・表現力（内容）】（各5点）

1. Batteries are at the (　　　　) of everyday mobile devices, such as smartphones, tablets and laptop computers.

2. The renewable energy sources may not be able to produce enough electricity when it is most needed. So, batteries are helpful to (　　　　) electricity.

3. Rechargeable batteries can (　　　　) to saving the environment.

Part 3

教科書 p.126〜p.127

/54

A Write the English words to match the Japanese. 【知識・技能（語彙）】(各2点)

1. .... 图 化学物質 B1
2. .... 图 銅 B2
3. .... 動 …を充電する
4. .... 图 鉛 A2
5. .... 图 酸 B2
6. .... 形 有害な A2

B Choose the word whose stressed syllable is different from the other three.

【知識・技能（発音）】(各2点)

1. ア．chem-i-cal-ly   イ．e-lec-tri-cal   ウ．en-vi-ron-ment   エ．re-charge-a-ble
2. ア．con-sist   イ．de-vice   ウ．in-vent   エ．met-al
3. ア．bat-ter-y   イ．de-vel-op   ウ．lith-i-um   エ．typ-i-cal

C Complete the following English sentences to match the Japanese.

【知識・技能（表現・文法）】(完答・各3点)

1. 結果的に，そのプロジェクトは計画どおりにはいかなかった。

   (   ) (   ) (   ), the project did not go as planned.
2. 祇園祭の起源は平安時代にさかのぼる。

   The origin of the Gion Festival (   ) (   ) (   ) the Heian period.
3. 携帯電話は衰退し，スマートフォンが優勢になった。

   Cellphones have declined and smartphones have (   ) (   ).

D Arrange the words in the proper order to match the Japanese.

【知識・技能（表現・文法）】(各4点)

1. この本は5章で構成されている。

   (chapters / consists / five / of / this book).

   ----
2. ニューヨーク市は Big Apple と呼ばれる。

   (call / New York City / people / the Big Apple).

   ----
3. 運動不足は私たちの健康を害する。

   (exercise / harmful / health / is / lack / of / our / to).

E Fill in each blank with a suitable word from the passage. 【思考力・判断力・表現力（内容）】(各5点)

1. Many different chemicals can be used in batteries and, (   ) speaking, they determine a battery's power.
2. The battery Volta developed could produce electricity but it couldn't (   ) for reuse.
3. The lead-acid battery, which was invented in 1859, is still widely used in (   ).

Part 4　教科書 p.130〜p.131　/54

A　Write the English words to match the Japanese.　【知識・技能（語彙）】（各2点）

1. _____ 副 商業的に
2. _____ 動 破裂する B2
3. _____ 動 …を採用する B1
4. _____ 形 安定した B1
5. _____ 名 未知の物
6. _____ 名 可能性 B1

B　Choose the word whose underlined part's sound is different from the other three.

【知識・技能（発音）】（各2点）

1. ア．adopt　　イ．explode　　ウ．oxide　　エ．possibility
2. ア．enable　　イ．safety　　ウ．stable　　エ．usable
3. ア．evolution　イ．plug　　ウ．result　　エ．unknown

C　Complete the following English sentences to match the Japanese.

【知識・技能（表現・文法）】（完答・各3点）

1. 彼女は新製品の開発での努力を評価された。

   She was (　　　　) (　　　　) her effort in developing a new product.

2. たき火をするときは，火がつきやすい乾いた枝を使いなさい。

   When you have a bonfire, use dry sticks that (　　　　) (　　　　) easily.

3. 私たちはピクニックに出かけたが，午後から寒くなってきた。さらに悪いことには，その後，雨が降り始めた。

   We went out for a picnic, but it became cold in the afternoon. (　　　　) (　　　　)
   (　　　　) (　　　　), it then started to rain.

D　Arrange the words in the proper order to match the Japanese.

【知識・技能（表現・文法）】（各4点）

1. その科学者は宇宙の謎を解くために大きく一歩前進した。

   The scientist (a / big / forward / made / solve / step / to) the mysteries of the universe.

2. その2か国は平和への活路を開くだろう。

   The (clear / countries / for / peace / the way / two / will).

3. 再生可能エネルギーは，その問題を解決するのに重要な役割を果たすだろう。

   Renewable energy (an / important / in / play / role / solving / will) the problem.

E　Fill in each blank with a suitable word from the passage.【思考力・判断力・表現力（内容）】（各5点）

1. Yoshino made the battery safe and (　　　　) usable for the first time.
2. Yoshino (　　　　) Goodenough's idea, but he used carbon on the other end of the battery.
3. Lithium-ion technology is still full of (　　　　) and (　　　　).

Activity Plus 教科書 p.134〜p.135 ／54

A Write the English words to match the Japanese. 【知識・技能（語彙）】（各2点）

1. ＿＿＿＿＿＿ 形 不安な, 心配な A2　　2. ＿＿＿＿＿＿ 動 …を放送する B2

3. ＿＿＿＿＿＿ 形 普及した B1　　4. ＿＿＿＿＿＿ 動 …を構成する B1

5. ＿＿＿＿＿＿ 動 …を刺激する B2　　6. ＿＿＿＿＿＿ 動 …を育む B2

B Choose the word whose stressed syllable is different from the other three.

【知識・技能（発音）】（各2点）

1. ア. a-ward　　イ. com-pose　　ウ. nour-ish　　エ. un-known

2. ア. broad-cast　　イ. re-place　　ウ. stor-age　　エ. wide-spread

3. ア. cur-rent-ly　　イ. in-ter-view　　ウ. ef-fi-cient　　エ. stim-u-late

C Complete the following English sentences to match the Japanese.

【知識・技能（表現・文法）】（完答・各3点）

1. 初めて彼に会ったとき, あなたはどう感じましたか。

   (　　　　) (　　　　) you (　　　　) when you first met him?

2. 水は人間の体の大部分を構成している。

   Water (　　　　) the major portion of the human body.

3. 毎日英語を使えば, 英語を話すのがもっと上手になりますよ。

   If you use English every day, you will become (　　　　) (　　　　) (　　　　) it.

D Arrange the words in the proper order to match the Japanese.

【知識・技能（表現・文法）】（各4点）

1. クラスの前でスピーチをするのは私を不安にした。

   Giving a speech (front / in / made / me / of / the class / uneasy).

   ＿＿＿＿＿＿＿＿＿＿＿＿＿＿＿＿＿＿＿＿＿＿

2. 運動は骨の成長を刺激し, 身長が伸びるのを助ける。

   Exercise (and / bone / growth / helps / increase / stimulates) height.

   ＿＿＿＿＿＿＿＿＿＿＿＿＿＿＿＿＿＿＿＿＿＿

3. 留学に興味がある生徒へアドバイスをください。

   Please give (advice / are / in / interested / some / the students / to / who) studying abroad.

   ＿＿＿＿＿＿＿＿＿＿＿＿＿＿＿＿＿＿＿＿＿＿

E Fill in each blank with a suitable word from the passage.

【思考力・判断力・表現力（内容）】（各5点）

1. Yoshino felt (　　　　) about the English interview on the phone.

2. Yoshino believes (　　　　) batteries in electric cars can help greatly.

3. Yoshino says that young people should look for and nourish a seed of (　　　　).

総合問題

　　/36

Read the following passage and answer the questions below.

Batteries, (ア)particular rechargeable ones, are essential in our daily lives.　What technological advances have been made in the history of batteries?

　Batteries are now a large part of our lives.　They are at the heart of everyday mobile devices, such as smartphones, tablets and laptop computers.　(A)Hybrid and electric cars would not exist without powerful batteries.　Innovations in batteries have had a great impact (　1　) the success of new technologies.

　Good rechargeable batteries are necessary (B)(efficient / in / make / of / order / to / use) renewable energy sources, such as sunlight and wind.　These energy sources depend highly (　2　) the weather, and they may not be able to produce enough electricity when it is most needed.　This is when batteries come (　3　) play: they store electricity until it is needed.

　Rechargeable batteries can contribute to (イ)save the environment.　Currently, single-use primary batteries occupy most of the market.　They are used only once and are then (ウ)throw (　4　).　Billions of such batteries become waste every year, and most of them end (　5　) in landfills.　(　6　) contrast, rechargeable batteries can be reused many times, and (C)this lessens the waste problem of primary batteries.　(D)Rechargeable batteries are becoming more important as a means to achieve a sustainable, greener future.

1.　下線部(ア)〜(ウ)の語を適切な形に変えなさい。　　　【知識・技能（表現・文法）】（各2点）

　　(ア) ....　　(イ) ....　　(ウ) ....

2.　下線部(A), (D)を日本語に訳しなさい。　　　【知識・技能（文法）】（各4点）

　　(A) ....

　　(D) ....

3.　下線部(B)の (　　) 内の語を適切に並べかえなさい。　　　【知識・技能（文法）】（4点）

　　..

4.　空所(1)〜(6)に入る適切な語を語群から選んで書きなさい。　　　【知識・技能（語彙・表現）】（各2点）

　　(1)(　　　　　)　(2)(　　　　　)　(3)(　　　　　)　(4)(　　　　　)

　　(5)(　　　　　)　(6)(　　　　　)

　　〔 at, away, for, in, into, of, on, up 〕

5.　下線部(C)this が指す内容を日本語で説明しなさい。　　　【思考力・判断力・表現力（内容）】（6点）

　　..

63

ディクテーション

Listen to the English and write down what you hear.

Part 1

You have bought a brand-new smartwatch. You are reading the user manual to find out how to (1.   ) the watch.

STEP 1

  Connect the USB plug of the battery charger to the port of an AC (2.   ).

STEP 2

  Place the watch on the charger. Make sure that it touches the charging pins. If the watch is (3.   ) connected, the charging icon will appear on the watch screen. If you cannot see the icon, you will need to check the contact between the charger and the watch.

STEP 3

  When the watch fully charges, "100%" will be (4.   ) on the watch screen and the watch will automatically stop charging. It takes about one hour for the watch to charge fully.

Notes:

  The proper temperature range for charging is between 10°C and 30°C. The watch may not charge properly below or above these temperatures.

  The charger has been developed (5.   ) for this product. The use of an unauthorized charger may damage the watch.

  Do not try to change the battery in the watch. The battery is built-in and should be replaced only at an authorized service center.

Part 2

Batteries, particularly rechargeable ones, are essential in our daily lives. What technological advances have been made in the history of batteries?

1 Batteries are now a large part of our lives. They are at the heart of everyday (1.   ) devices, such as smartphones, tablets and laptop computers. Hybrid and (2.   ) cars would not exist without powerful batteries. Innovations in batteries have had a great impact on the success of new technologies.

2 Good rechargeable batteries are necessary in order to make (3.   ) use of renewable energy sources, such as sunlight and wind. These energy sources depend highly on the weather, and they may not be able to produce enough electricity when it is most needed. This is when batteries come into play: they store electricity until it is needed.

3 Rechargeable batteries can contribute to saving the environment. Currently, single-use primary batteries (4.   ) most of the market. They are used only once and are then thrown away. Billions of such batteries become waste every year, and most of them end up in landfills. In contrast, rechargeable batteries can be reused many times, and this lessens the waste problem of primary batteries. Rechargeable batteries are becoming more important as a (5.   ) to achieve a sustainable, greener future.

Part 3

4 What does a typical battery consist of? It has two (1.   ) ends and a chemical between them. These parts (2.   ) with each other inside the battery. As a result, electricity is produced. Many different chemicals can be used in batteries

and, generally speaking, they determine a battery's power.

⑤ The word "battery" goes back to the 18th century. It was first used by Benjamin Franklin of the U.S. He called a device he invented an "electrical battery." It could only store electricity. In 1800, Alessandro Volta of Italy developed a "true" battery. He used copper, zinc and salt water in his device, and his battery could produce electricity (3.   ). However, it couldn't recharge for reuse.

⑥ The earliest rechargeable battery was the lead-acid battery. It was invented in 1859. This type is still widely used in cars. In 1899, nickel-cadmium batteries were created, and they were a top choice for use in portable devices for many years. In the 1990s, nickel-metal (4.   ) batteries took over. They had a longer life. They were also less harmful to the environment. Later, as people wanted smaller and better batteries, lithium-ion batteries were developed.

Part 4

⑦ The 2019 Nobel Prize in Chemistry went to Japanese scientist Akira Yoshino. He shared the prize with John B. Goodenough of the U.S. and Britain's Stanley Whittingham. They were recognized for their work on the lithium-ion battery (LIB). Yoshino made the battery safe and (1.   ) usable for the first time.

⑧ The lithium-based battery was invented by Whittingham in the 1970s. However, his battery did not last very long. To make matters worse, it also had a serious safety concern, as it could catch fire and (2.   ). In the 1980s, a more powerful type was developed by Goodenough. He used lithium-cobalt oxide on one end of the battery. Some years later, Yoshino made a step further. He (3.   ) Goodenough's idea, but he used carbon on the other end. This cleared the way for a safe, (4.   ) and practical LIB.

⑨ The LIB is one of the most common batteries today. Its evolution does not stop, and many important discoveries continue to be made. Lithium-ion technology is still full of unknowns and (5.   ). Yoshino believes that the LIB can play a central role in creating a society without fossil fuels. LIB technology is bringing great power to people around the world.

Activity Plus

You are listening to Akira Yoshino speaking shortly after the announcement of his Nobel Prize in Chemistry.

Q1) How did you feel when you heard you were awarded the prize?

I couldn't believe the news, and it didn't feel real at first. On the phone, I had an interview in English. Actually, I felt uneasy about it because I thought my English interview would be (1.   ) around the world.

Q2) How can the lithium-ion battery help a society based on renewable energy?

I believe lithium-ion batteries in electric cars can help greatly. Our future society needs a better power storage system. If electric cars become widespread, they can (2.   ) a huge power storage system. That will (3.   ) the use of solar and wind power.

Q3) What message do you have for young people who are interested in science?

You should look for and (4.   ) a seed of interest. In my case, it was a book about candles. When I read it, I thought chemistry was fascinating. That experience has led to my work on the lithium-ion battery. When you get interested in something and work toward it, you will become better at it.

Part 1 教科書 p.140〜p.141   /54

A Write the English words to match the Japanese. 【知識・技能（語彙）】（各2点）

1. ＿＿＿＿＿＿ 图 地主
2. ＿＿＿＿＿＿ 動 …に似ている B1
3. ＿＿＿＿＿＿ 图 哲学者 B1
4. ＿＿＿＿＿＿ 图 危機 B1
5. ＿＿＿＿＿＿ 图 出来事 B1
6. ＿＿＿＿＿＿ 图 対策, 処置 B1

B Choose the word whose underlined part's sound is different from the other three. 【知識・技能（発音）】（各2点）

1. ア. be<u>h</u>alf   イ. de<u>c</u>line   ウ. re<u>s</u>emble   エ. re<u>s</u>triction
2. ア. l<u>o</u>ckdown   イ. phil<u>o</u>sopher   ウ. pr<u>o</u>perty   エ. unf<u>o</u>rtunately
3. ア. cr<u>i</u>sis   イ. f<u>i</u>nally   ウ. pr<u>i</u>vate   エ. s<u>o</u>cial

C Complete the following English sentences to match the Japanese. 【知識・技能（表現・文法）】（各3点）

1. 来週，英語のテストがあります。だから，英語の勉強を懸命にしています。
   We have an English exam next week. That's (　　　) we study English hard.
2. どうしてこんな結果が生じたのか，私たちは話し合った。
   We talked about how this result (　　　) about.
3. 生徒会を代表して，彼はスピーチをしました。
   On (　　　) of school council, he made a speech.

D Arrange the words in the proper order to match the Japanese. 【知識・技能（表現・文法）】（各4点）

1. 彼は英語だけでなくフランス語も話すことができる。
   He can speak (also / but / English / French / not / only).

2. たくさんの観光客が車をとめるので，その道はふさがっていた。
   Many tourists (blocked / cars / parked / the road / with).

3. 私はその道の真ん中に彼が立っているのを見ました。
   I saw (him / in / middle / of / standing / the) the road.

E Fill in each blank with a suitable word from the passage. 【思考力・判断力・表現力（内容）】（各5点）

1. In the (　　　), the worst result has come about.
2. We need to take (　　　) before similar incidents happen.
3. The "Philosophy Tree" leaned (　　　) one side in the middle of a field.

Part 2　教科書 p.142〜p.143　　　/54

A　Write the English words to match the Japanese.　【知識・技能（語彙）】（各2点）

1. ....　图 制限，規制 B2
2. ....　图 衰退，衰え B1
3. ....　形 伝染性の B2
4. ....　图 目的地 B1
5. ....　形 度を越えた B2
6. ....　图 居住者 B2

B　Choose the word whose stressed syllable is different from the other three.

【知識・技能（発音）】（各2点）

1. ア．chem-is-try　　イ．in-ci-dent　　ウ．in-fec-tious　　エ．us-a-ble
2. ア．de-pend-ent　　イ．re-sem-ble　　ウ．res-i-dent　　エ．re-stric-tion
3. ア．al-ti-tude　　イ．at-ti-tude　　ウ．ex-ces-sive　　エ．stim-u-late

C　Complete the following English sentences to match the Japanese.

【知識・技能（表現・文法）】（各3点）

1. 彼らはどのようにストレスに対処するかを話し合っている。

   They are talking about how they can (　　　　) with their stress.

2. かつて彼女は看護師になりたかったが諦めた。

   At (　　　　) time she wanted to be a nurse, but gave it up.

3. 彼らが警報を発する前に，私たちはその問題を話し合わなければならない。

   We should discuss the issue before they raise the (　　　　).

D　Arrange the words in the proper order to match the Japanese.

【知識・技能（表現・文法）】（各4点）

1. 彼女は食べ物やお金を娘に頼っている。

   She (dependent / food and money / for / her daughter / is / on).

   ----

2. 彼らはこれらの問題を社会問題だと定義しました。

   They (as / defined / social issues / these problems).

   ----

3. 彼はその課題を解決できるかどうかと考えている。

   He (can / he / if / is / solve / that problem / wondering).

E　Fill in each blank with a suitable word from the passage.

【思考力・判断力・表現力（内容）】（各5点）

1. (　　　　) fact, we still remember the number of tourists decreased drastically in 2020.
2. Sightseeing places were (　　　　) longer able to cope with their own popularity.
3. The Oxford Dictionary chose "overtourism" (　　　　) one of its Words of the Year.

Part 3

教科書 p.144〜p.145

/54

A Write the English words to match the Japanese.　【知識・技能（語彙）】（各2点）

1. .... 名 ストライキ A2
2. .... 名 高度，標高 B2
3. .... 名 遅れ，遅延 A2
4. .... 名 混雑
5. .... 名 不便
6. .... 動 通勤［通学］する B2

B Choose the word whose underlined part's sound is different from the other three.

【知識・技能（発音）】（各2点）

1. ア．comm<u>u</u>te 　イ．f<u>u</u>ture 　ウ．res<u>u</u>lt 　エ．<u>u</u>sable
2. ア．cl<u>ou</u>d 　イ．d<u>ou</u>bt 　ウ．inb<u>ou</u>nd 　エ．w<u>ou</u>nd
3. ア．<u>a</u>ttraction 　イ．d<u>a</u>mage 　ウ．d<u>a</u>nger 　エ．dem<u>a</u>nd

C Complete the following English sentences to match the Japanese.

【知識・技能（表現・文法）】（各3点）

1. 私の弟は半年間運転を禁じられた。

   My brother was banned (　　　　) driving for six months.
2. 私はお金を貯めるのに苦労しています。

   I have trouble (　　　　) money.
3. 私の母は働き過ぎによる疲れが原因で亡くなった。

   My mother died from fatigue caused (　　　　) overwork.

D Arrange the words in the proper order to match the Japanese.

【知識・技能（表現・文法）】（各4点）

1. あのピンクの家は彼が住んでいる家です。

   That pink house (he / in / is / lives / the house / which).

   ----
2. 選挙の結果が抗議につながる可能性があると言われている。

   It is said that (can / lead / of / protests / the election / the result / to).

   ----
3. 私は間食をしないようにしている。

   I make (a rule / avoid / between / eating / it / meals / snacks / to).

E Fill in each blank with a suitable word from the passage.

【思考力・判断力・表現力（内容）】（各5点）

1. Some climbers have died (　　　　) altitude sickness on Mt. Everest.
2. Workers at the Louvre Museum went (　　　　) strike.
3. Inbound tourism contributed greatly (　　　　) the Japanese economy.

A　Write the English words to match the Japanese.　【知識・技能（語彙）】（各2点）

1. .... 图 教授 B1
2. .... 形 責任のある B1
3. .... 動 …と言う B1
4. .... 動 …を必要とする B1
5. .... 動 …を最大にする
6. .... 形 有益な B2

B　Choose the word whose stressed syllable is different from the other three.　【知識・技能（発音）】（各2点）

1. ア．ben-e-fi-cial　イ．com-mer-cial-ly　ウ．phi-los-o-pher　エ．re-spon-si-ble
2. ア．bal-ance　イ．dam-age　ウ．de-mand　エ．per-fect
3. ア．climb-er　イ．ef-fort　ウ．head-line　エ．re-mark

C　Complete the following English sentences to match the Japanese.　【知識・技能（表現・文法）】（各3点）

1. 今こそ，その問題について議論すべきときです。

   Now is the time (　　　　) we should discuss that issue.
2. 私たちの本当の目標は何か，よく考えるべきだ。

   We should reflect (　　　　) what our real goals are.
3. あなたがアメリカに住むことを想像してみて。

   Imagine (　　　　) you live in America.

D　Arrange the words in the proper order to match the Japanese.　【知識・技能（表現・文法）】（各4点）

1. 彼女が昨日会ったのはトムでした。

   It (met / she / that / Tom / was / yesterday).

   ----
2. その問題を解ける人は誰もいない。

   There (can / is / no / person / problem / solve / that / who).

   ----
3. 昨夜，その家が焼け落ちるのを見た。

   I (burned / down / saw / that house / was) last night.

E　Fill in each blank with a suitable word from the passage.　【思考力・判断力・表現力（内容）】（各5点）

1. It is (　　　　) to us to make sure traveling stays a beneficial experience.
2. Responsible tourism demands responsibility (　　　　) achieving sustainable development.
3. We can maximize the positive effects and minimize the negative (　　　　).

Activity Plus 教科書 p.152〜p.153

/54

A Write the English words to match the Japanese. 【知識・技能（語彙）】（各2点）

1. .... 图 発言，意見 A2
2. .... 形 重大な，ゆゆしき B2
3. .... 形 …に値する B1
4. .... 图 風潮，傾向 B1
5. .... 接 しかも，その上 B1
6. .... 图 結論 B1

B Choose the word whose underlined part's sound is different from the other three.

【知識・技能（発音）】（各2点）

1. ア．smoo<u>th</u>　　イ．wea<u>th</u>er　　ウ．wor<u>th</u>　　エ．wor<u>th</u>y

2. ア．con<u>c</u>lusion　イ．<u>cr</u>ucial　　ウ．introd<u>u</u>ce　エ．r<u>u</u>de

3. ア．c<u>a</u>lm　　　イ．ex<u>a</u>ct　　　ウ．fr<u>a</u>nkly　エ．im<u>ag</u>ine

C Complete the following English sentences to match the Japanese.

【知識・技能（表現・文法）】（各3点）

1. 私たちは彼の決断に同意できません。

   We can't agree (　　　　　) his decision.

2. 私の意見は彼の意見とは異なっています。

   My opinion is different (　　　　　) his.

3. クラスのみんながチームの成功に貢献した。

   Everyone in the class contributed (　　　　　) the team's success.

D Arrange the words in the proper order to match the Japanese.

【知識・技能（表現・文法）】（各4点）

1. 私たちは英語の勉強をするという目的でここに来ました。

   We (came / English / for / here / of / purpose / studying / the).

   ----

2. 彼が勧めてくれた本は読む価値がある。

   The (book / he / is / reading / recommended / worth).

   ----

3. 私たちはどこへいつ行ったらよいのか知りたい。

   We (and when / go / know / to / to / want / where).

E Fill in each blank with a suitable word from the passage.

【思考力・判断力・表現力（内容）】（各5点）

1. (　　　　　) conclusion, Mika doesn't agree with the statement.
2. Many people travel for the purpose (　　　　) taking great pictures.
3. People should not post photos of their trips (　　　　) social media.

総合問題

/40

Read the following passage and answer the questions below.

　　At one time, overtourism was making headlines all over the world.　In Barcelona, residents protested （　1　） many problems caused by having too many tourists.　In Paris, workers at the Louvre Museum went on (A)(conditions / dangerous / from / having / many visitors / resulting / strike over / too).　In Venice, residents (B)(banned / cruise ships / docking / from / hard / there / to get / tried).　On Mt. Everest, some climbers have died of altitude sickness （　2　） the delays caused by too many climbers.

　　How about in Japan?　The number of tourists coming to this country was once increasing rapidly.　Inbound tourism contributed greatly to the Japanese economy. Having too many visitors, （　3　）, can lead to many problems, such as noise, litter and traffic congestion.　It can cause great inconvenience to local residents.　It may even spoil the attraction of the sightseeing spot itself.

　　In Kyoto, people were feeling the negative impacts of overtourism.　For example, they had trouble boarding the buses （　4　） they commute.　One of the local residents expressed his mixed feelings: "Many locals depend on tourism, （　5　） I'm not saying we don't need tourists.　But we do see its negative impacts."　Even Japanese tourists avoided visiting Kyoto because of overtourism.

1.　空所(1), (2), (3), (4), (5)に入る適切な語（句）を選びなさい。　【知識・技能（語彙・表現）】(各4点)

(1)　ア．against　　　　イ．for　　　　　　ウ．of　　　　　　エ．with

(2)　ア．because of　　イ．for example　　ウ．in addition　　エ．on behalf of

(3)　ア．however　　　イ．instead　　　　ウ．so　　　　　　エ．therefore

(4)　ア．by which　　　イ．in which　　　ウ．of which　　　エ．which

(5)　ア．because　　　イ．but　　　　　　ウ．however　　　エ．so

2.　下線部(A), (B)の（　　）内の語句を適切に並べかえなさい。　【知識・技能（文法）】(各5点)

(A) ---

(B) ---

3.　本文の内容に合っているものをすべて選びなさい。　【思考力・判断力・表現力（内容）】(完答・10点)

ア．Having too many visitors in Japan may damage the attraction of sightseeing spots.

イ．In Paris, workers at the Louvre Museum went on strike because of overtourism.

ウ．Inbound tourism contributed greatly to the Japanese economy.

エ．In Barcelona, people are happy to have many tourists.

オ．In Venice, residents can get cruise ships banned easily from docking there.

ディクテーション

Listen to the English and write down what you hear.

Part 1

You are reading a blog post about a famous tree in Hokkaido which was very popular among tourists.

I have to tell you a very disappointing thing.　Unfortunately, a famous tree on a farm in Biei, Hokkaido, was finally cut down by the landowner.　This tree, (1.　　　　) far to one side in the middle of a field, (2.　　　　) a philosopher in deep thought.　That is why it came to be called the "Philosophy Tree."

(3.　　　　), the owner could not work on his farm because of tourists blocking the road with their parked cars.　More and more tourists entered his private land to get the best shots on their smartphones, and they damaged his crops.　They ignored (4.　　　　) signs saying, "PRIVATE PROPERTY: NO ENTRY."　The signs were written not only in Japanese and English but also in Chinese and Korean.

I, and maybe other people in Japan, too, felt a sense of (5.　　　　).　On behalf of the bloggers in Japan, I wrote about it on this blog.　In the end, the worst result has come about and I am shocked.　I am afraid that similar (6.　　　　) with tourists may happen in other popular areas in the future.　What can we do to prevent this?　What measures should we take?

Part 2

Do you want to travel abroad?　With a (1.　　　　) on non-essential travel and complete lockdown in some countries, we were able to witness what could happen to the world.

①　Recently, tourism has gone through some (2.　　　　) due to infectious diseases and natural disasters.　In fact, it is still fresh in our memory that the number of tourists decreased (3.　　　　) in 2020 due to the influence of COVID-19.　However, do you remember that tourists were visiting various spots in large numbers at one time?

②　Overtourism quickly became one of the most serious social problems in the modern age of travel.　More and more people visited sightseeing places, thanks to cheaper air (4.　　　　), rising incomes and the power of social media.　These places were no longer able to cope with their own popularity.　In the past few years, a number of (5.　　　　) have raised the alarm over this situation.

③　In 2018, the Oxford Dictionary chose "overtourism" as one of its Words of the Year. The World Tourism Organization defined it as "the negative impact that tourism has on a destination."　An excess of tourist (6.　　　　) impacted the local people's quality of life.　Excessive crowds hindered the experiences of the tourists themselves.　Many places dependent on money from tourism wondered if they could maintain a good environment not only for travelers but also for their own residents.

Part 3

④　At one time, overtourism was making (1.　　　　) all over the world.　In Barcelona, residents protested against many problems caused by having too many tourists.　In Paris, workers at the Louvre Museum went on strike over dangerous conditions resulting from having too many visitors.　In Venice, residents tried hard to get cruise ships (2.　　　　) from docking there.　On Mt. Everest, some climbers have died of altitude sickness because of the (3.　　　　) caused by too many climbers.

⑤　How about in Japan?　The number of tourists coming to this country was once increasing rapidly.　Inbound tourism contributed greatly to the Japanese economy. Having too many visitors, however, can lead to many problems, such as noise, litter and traffic (4.   ). It can cause great inconvenience to local residents. It may even spoil the attraction of the sightseeing spot itself.

6 In Kyoto, people were feeling the negative impacts of overtourism. For example, they had trouble boarding the buses by which they (5.   ). One of the local residents expressed his mixed feelings: "Many locals depend on tourism, so I'm not saying we don't need tourists. But we do see its negative impacts." Even Japanese tourists avoided visiting Kyoto because of overtourism.

Part 4

7 Now is the time when we should (1.   ) on what it actually means to travel. Imagine that you are a resident of a famous tourist destination. Do you think people in your town want to welcome more tourists from abroad? Do you think foreign tourists who visit your town will come back again in the future?

8 Professor Harold Goodwin, who wrote *Responsible Tourism*, (2.   ), "Tourism is like a fire —— you can use it to cook your food or it can burn your house down." Responsible tourism is about making places better for people to live in and better for people to visit. It (3.   ) responsibility for achieving sustainable development.

9 How can we achieve responsible tourism to overcome the problems of overtourism? There is no single perfect solution to these problems. There are, however, many ways to reduce crowding and protect the environment. It is by taking a more responsible approach to tourism that we can (4.   ) the positive effects and minimize the negative ones. We all live on this beautiful planet and we are in the same boat. Traveling should be a (5.   ) experience. It is up to us to make sure it stays that way.

Activity Plus

In your class, you are listening to a discussion of the following (1.   ): "In order to prevent overtourism, people should not post pictures of their trips on social media."

Teacher: As we have learned, overtourism has become a (2.   ) problem in many places. When people make a decision about where to visit and when, they depend greatly on the information they see on social media. So for today's discussion, let's talk about the statement, "In order to prevent overtourism, people should not post pictures of their trips on social media." What's your opinion, Satoshi?

Satoshi: Frankly, I disagree with this statement. Many people want to travel for the purpose of taking great pictures and showing them online. I think it's a good thing. If you don't get hundreds of likes on your posts, is it even (3.   ) going? If you don't have any good pictures to post on social media, will you still go traveling? I wouldn't. How about you, Emily?

Emily: Well, I'm afraid that traveling has become a photo contest for many tourists. Wherever I travel, I see the growing (4.   ) of "doing it for social media." It's all about who can get the best shots, and it's all evaluated by the number of likes and followers you have. So I agree with this statement. Now, it's your turn, Mika.

Mika: My idea is different from Emily's. I believe that social media can contribute to helping with "undertourism." That is the movement for attracting people to less-visited places that need more attention. (5.   ), I think social media are not the only reason for overtourism. In conclusion, I don't agree with this statement.

Part 1 　教科書 p.158〜p.159 　　/54

A Write the English words to match the Japanese. 　【知識・技能（語彙）】（各2点）

1. ....　動 …を無理やりに引っ張り出す B1　2. ....　名 サイン

3. ....　名 枠 A2　4. ....　形 想像上の, 架空の

5. ....　形 勝ち誇った, 得意になった　6. ....　形 理解力がある

B Choose the word whose stressed syllable is different from the other three.

【知識・技能（発音）】（各2点）

1. ア. ac-com-plish　イ. au-to-graph　ウ. do-min-ion　エ. re-cep-tive

2. ア. con-stant-ly　イ. con-ti-nent　ウ. neg-a-tive　エ. tri-um-phant

3. ア. e-co-nom-ic　イ. es-pe-cial-ly　ウ. im-pe-ri-al　エ. so-ci-e-ty

C Complete the following English sentences to match the Japanese.

【知識・技能（表現・文法）】（完答・各3点）

1. 私はあなたを3時間も待っているのですよ。冗談じゃないわ！

　I've been waiting for you for three hours; (　　　　) kidding!

2. どんなことがあってもだれが何と言っても，私は英語を勉強し続けます。

　Nothing and nobody can (　　　　) (　　　　) (　　　　) studying English.

3. トムは，昨年初めて出会って以来ずっとメアリーに恋しています。

　Tom has been (　　　　) (　　　　) (　　　　) Mary since he first met her last year.

D Arrange the words in the proper order to match the Japanese.

【知識・技能（表現・文法）】（各4点）

1. その本のことは聞いたことはありますが，読んだことはありません。

　(but / heard / I've / I've never / of / the book,) read it.

　--

2. あなたはこの仕事で少なくとも時給1,000円もらえるでしょう。

　You will be able to get (1,000 yen / an hour / at / for / least / this job).

　--

3. 親は学校で起こることをいつも知っているとは限らない。

　Parents (always / don't / goes / know / on / what) at school.

　--

E Fill in each blank with a suitable word from the passage.

【思考力・判断力・表現力（内容）】（各5点）

1. Wendy and I are here to get Craig the Cat's (　　　　).

2. He is a famous rock star, and Wendy is (　　　) (　　　) (　　　) him.

3. I'm sure she cannot know his (　　　) (　　　), but now she is standing up and is calling Craig the Cat in one of the rooms from a lobby phone.

Part 2 教科書 p.160〜p.161 ／54

A Write the English words to match the Japanese. 【知識・技能（語彙）】（各2点）

1. .... 图 受話器　　　2. .... 图 機密漏洩 B2

3. .... 代 何一つ…ない B1　4. .... 图 （見晴らしのきく）有利な位置

5. .... 图 入札者，競り手　6. .... 動 ため息をつく B2

B Choose the word whose stressed syllable is different from the other three.

【知識・技能（発音）】（各2点）

1. ア. af-fect　　イ. gui-tar　　ウ. pro-tect　　エ. van-tage

2. ア. col-lege　イ. may-be　　ウ. un-ion　　　エ. un-til

3. ア. a-bol-ish　イ. com-put-er　ウ. de-li-cious　エ. man-ag-er

C Complete the following English sentences to match the Japanese.

【知識・技能（表現・文法）】（完答・各3点）

1. 電話の向こう側でだれかが受話器をとったが，一言も言わなかった。

Someone picked up the phone on (　　　) (　　　) (　　　), but there was only silence.

2. 私は，世界中を旅した男性がいるのを知っています。

I know (　　　) a man who traveled all over the world.

3. 彼女をひとりにしておいてあげなさい。プロジェクトのための新しいアイディアを考えているのですから。

(　　　) her (　　　). She is thinking of new ideas for a project.

D Arrange the words in the proper order to match the Japanese. 【知識・技能（表現・文法）】（各4点）

1. 私は彼に二度と電話しないでと言って，電話を切りました。

I told him never (again, / and / call / hung / me / to / up).

2. その少女は待ちくたびれた様子だ。

The girl seems (be / of / tired / to / waiting).

3. 彼はあそこで何をしているの？

(doing / he / is / over / there / what)?

E Fill in each blank with a suitable word from the passage. 【思考力・判断力・表現力（内容）】（各5点）

1. The woman who answers the phone is Craig's (　　　), who is his manager.

2. She tells Wendy that she will not get his autograph and she (　　　) up.

3. Wendy says we'll just have to wait until he goes into the hotel (　　　) (　　　) to eat.

Part 3 　教科書 p.162～p.163

/54

A　Write the English words to match the Japanese.　【知識・技能 (語彙)】(各2点)

1. .... 形 やせた, 身の締まった B1　2. .... 動 ささやく, 小声で話す B2
3. .... 形 普通の, ありふれた B1　4. .... 動 じろじろ見る, じっと見つめる B1
5. .... 動 向ける, 照準する B2　6. .... 動 身体を曲げる, かがむ A2

B　Choose the word whose stressed syllable is different from the other three.

【知識・技能 (発音)】(各2点)

1. ア．ath-lete　　イ．head-ache　　ウ．ho-tel　　エ．spir-it
2. ア．con-fuse　　イ．con-tain　　ウ．e-lect　　エ．suf-fer
3. ア．cam-er-a　　イ．nor-mal-ly　　ウ．rep-re-sent　　エ．sud-den-ly

C　Complete the following English sentences to match the Japanese.

【知識・技能 (表現・文法)】(完答・各3点)

1. 私の前にだれかが立っているという気がして, 私は視線をあげました。

   I felt there was someone standing in front of me, so I looked (　　　　).
2. 3台のバスが通過して行きましたが, どれも私の乗るバスではありませんでした。

   Three buses passed (　　　), but none of them was the right one.
3. 私がこの前会ったとき, 彼は図書館に向かっていました。

   The last time I saw him, he was (　　　) (　　　　) the library.

D　Arrange the words in the proper order to match the Japanese.　【知識・技能 (表現・文法)】(各4点)

1. その男性は燃えている部屋に向かって水をかけた。

   The man (aimed / at / room / the burning / the water).

   ----

2. 私は机の下にペンを落とし, 拾い上げようとかがみ込みました。

   I (a pen / and / bent / down / dropped / the desk / under) to pick it up.

   ----

3. そこをどいていただけませんか。ショーが見えません。

   Would (get / of / out / please / the way / you)? I can't see the show.

E　Fill in each blank with a suitable word from the passage.　【思考力・判断力・表現力 (内容)】(各5点)

1. Wendy and I see an (　　　　) young guy is going to the hotel coffee shop with a woman.
2. Wendy (　　　　) them, and asks for his autograph. His mother says he is not Craig, and refuses her request.
3. Somebody with a (　　　) tries to take his photo.

Part 4 教科書 p.164〜p.165

/54

A Write the English words to match the Japanese. 【知識・技能（語彙）】（各2点）

1. .... 圏 シッシッ
2. .... 副 すぐに，直ちに B1
3. .... 動 大声を上げる B2
4. .... 形 上品な，高級な A2
5. .... 图 靴下，ソックス A2
6. .... 图 足首，くるぶし A2

B Choose the word whose underlined part's sound is different from the other three.

【知識・技能（発音）】（各2点）

1. ア．behind　　　イ．decide　　　ウ．figure　　　エ．hide
2. ア．creative　　　イ．stadium　　　ウ．says　　　エ．wave
3. ア．couple　　　イ．none　　　ウ．lucky　　　エ．socks

C Complete the following English sentences to match the Japanese.

【知識・技能（表現・文法）】（完答・各3点）

1. 彼は最も重要な試合で冷静さを失い，レッドカードをもらった。

He (　　　) (　　　) (　　　) in the most important game and got a red card.

2. その女の子たちは態度が悪くてレストランから追い出された。

The girls were (　　　) (　　　) (　　　) the restaurant because of their bad behavior.

3. そんなにどならないでよ。私は何も悪いことなんかしていないわ。

Don't (　　　) (　　　) me like that. I haven't done anything wrong.

D Arrange the words in the proper order to match the Japanese. 【知識・技能（表現・文法）】（各4点）

1. だれかが私の名前を呼んだと思ったので，だれかしらと振り向きました。

I thought that someone had called my name, so I (around / it / see / to / turned / was / who).

2. インターネット上に個人情報を公表してはいけません。

Don't (give / information / out / personal / your) on the Internet.

3. 最初のページに戻ってもう一度文章を読みましょう。

Let's (back / first / page / the / to / turn) and read the sentences again.

E Fill in each blank with a suitable word from the passage. 【思考力・判断力・表現力（内容）】（各5点）

1. Craig's mother angrily tells the (　　　) to leave.
2. When Wendy and I try to run out of the hotel, someone shouts, "(　　　)!"
3. Wendy tells Craig that she knows (　　　) about him because she is an (　　　) on him.

Part 5

教科書 p.166〜p.167

/54

A　Write the English words to match the Japanese.　【知識・技能 (語彙)】(各2点)

1. ＿＿＿＿＿＿＿　图 化粧, メーキャップ　2. ＿＿＿＿＿＿＿　動 …をだめにする, …を破壊する
3. ＿＿＿＿＿＿＿　图 畏敬の念, 畏怖 B2　4. ＿＿＿＿＿＿＿　動 大声を上げる, 怒鳴る B2
5. ＿＿＿＿＿＿＿　副 優しく, 好意的に　6. ＿＿＿＿＿＿＿　形 満足した

B　Choose the word whose underlined part's sound is different from the other three.

【知識・技能 (発音)】(各2点)

1. ア. feline　　イ. president　　ウ. wreck　　エ. yell
2. ア. brood　　イ. foot　　ウ. stood　　エ. wood
3. ア. awe　　イ. grow　　ウ. moment　　エ. poke

C　Complete the following English sentences to match the Japanese.

【知識・技能 (表現・文法)】(完答・各3点)

1. 彼女は与えられたリストから数冊の本を選び出しました。

She (　　) (　　) several books from the list she had been given.

2. もしあなたが心配しすぎたら, 結局あなたは何もしないでしょう。

If you worry too much, you'll (　　) (　　) doing nothing.

3. 部屋にいる全員が私をじっと見ているように思いました。

I thought everyone in the room was (　　) (　　) me.

D　Arrange the words in the proper order to match the Japanese.　【知識・技能 (表現・文法)】(各4点)

1. 私は最初は納豆が食べられませんでしたが, すぐに好きになりました。

At first I couldn't eat natto, but soon (got / I / it / like / to).

2. 近所の人たちみんなが私の母に畏敬の念を持っていました。

All of the neighbors were (awe / in / mother / my / of).

3. この問題はけっしてひとりでに消えてなくなりはしない。私たち自身で一生懸命解決に努めなければならない。

This problem will (away / by / go / itself / never). We ourselves must try hard to solve it.

E　Fill in each blank with a suitable word from the passage.

【思考力・判断力・表現力 (内容)】(完答・各5点)

1. Wendy tells Craig that she (　　) a lot about Craig the Cat and ended up thinking of him as her (　　).
2. Now Craig the Cat looks as if he is (　　) fan.
3. We are back in the hotel coffee shop, and the (　　) of us are sitting around a table.

78

総合問題

Read the following passage and answer the questions below.

　Craig's mother glares at the photographer. "Shoo!" she says, (A)wave her hand. "Shoo immediately!"

　The photographer leaves. (B)So does Wendy. She runs back to me. I am hiding behind a fern.

　Wendy has lost her cool. "Let's get out of here before we're kicked out or arrested," she says.

　We rush toward a door.

　"Wait!" Someone is yelling （　1　） us.

　When I hear the word *wait*, it's a signal for me to move even faster. But Wendy stops. "It's *him*!" she says, without turning around.

　I turn. It *is* Craig the Cat. He's alone. He rushes up to Wendy. "How did you know me?" he asks. "I didn't tell (C)(I / staying / the media / was / where). And I certainly didn't give out my room number. I wasn't wearing my cat costume. And I was with my mother. So （　2　）?"

　Wendy looks at me. She's trying (D)(answer / decide / if / she / should / to). Something in her wants to and something in her doesn't want to. She turns back to Craig. "I'm an expert on you," she says. "I know you like fancy, old hotels, and this is the oldest and the fanciest in town. I know your lucky number is twelve, so I figured you'd stay on the twelfth floor in room 1212. I know you always wear red socks when you're not performing, so tonight I watched ankles in the lobby. And I knew you'd be with your manager —— your mother."

1. 下線部(A)の語を適切な形に変えなさい。　【知識・技能（文法）】（6点）

　　（　　　　　　　　　　　　）

2. 下線部(B)の解釈として最も適当なものを選びなさい。　【思考力・判断力・表現力（内容）】（10点）

　　ア．Wendy glares at the photographer, too.　　イ．Wendy leaves, too.

　　ウ．Wendy runs back to me, too.　　エ．Wendy hides behind a fern, too.

3. 空所(1), (2)に入る適切な語を選びなさい。　【知識・技能（文法）】（各6点）

　　(1)　ア．at　　　　　イ．for　　　　　ウ．on　　　　　エ．toward

　　(2)　ア．how　　　　イ．what　　　　ウ．when　　　　エ．why

4. 下線部(C), (D)の（　　　）内の語句を適切に並べかえなさい。　【知識・技能（文法）】（各4点）

　　(C) --

　　(D) --

5. 本文の内容と合っていないものを選びなさい。　【思考力・判断力・表現力（内容）】（10点）

　　ア．Wendy knows from the voice that it is Craig the Cat that is yelling, "Wait!"

　　イ．Craig the Cat didn't give out where he was staying.

　　ウ．Craig the Cat was not wearing his cat costume.

　　エ．Wendy didn't know that Craig the Cat was with his mother, who was his manager.

79

Part 1 　教科書 p.174〜p.175 　　/54

A Write the English words to match the Japanese. 【知識・技能 (語彙)】(各2点)

1. .... 图 近所, 地区 B1
2. .... 形 木製の, 木でできた A2
3. .... 動 …を固定する B1
4. .... 副 しきりに, 熱心に B2
5. .... 副 どこかに A2
6. .... 動 …をしゃぶる, …を舐める B2

B Choose the word whose underlined part's sound is different from the other three.

【知識・技能 (発音)】(各2点)

1. ア. am<u>a</u>zing 　　イ. ch<u>a</u>mber 　　ウ. h<u>a</u>tred 　　エ. m<u>a</u>gic
2. ア. imm<u>e</u>diately 　イ. pr<u>e</u>cious 　　ウ. pr<u>e</u>judice 　エ. tog<u>e</u>ther
3. ア. bom<u>b</u> 　　　イ. fas<u>t</u>en 　　　ウ. laug<u>h</u>ter 　エ. mus<u>c</u>le

C Complete the following English sentences to match the Japanese.

【知識・技能 (表現・文法)】(完答・各3点)

1. 父は私に肩車をしてくれました。

   My father (　　　　) me (　　　　) on his shoulders.
2. 翌日, ティムは商用でパリに行きました。

   The next day, Tim went to Paris (　　　　) (　　　　).
3. その少女は何時間もおもちゃで遊んだ。

   The little girl amused (　　　　) (　　　　) her toys for hours.

D Arrange the words in the proper order to match the Japanese. 【知識・技能 (表現・文法)】(各4点)

1. 郵便局の隣には, 小さな灰色の教会が立っている。

   (a little / beside / post office / stands / the) gray church.

   ----
2. 彼は自分が何でも知っていると思っている。

   He thinks there is (does / he / know / not / nothing).

   ----
3. ここには私の仕事はないようだ。

   There (any work / be / doesn't / seem / to) for me here.

E Fill in each blank with a suitable word from the passage. 【思考力・判断力・表現力 (内容)】(各5点)

1. When I was a small child, we had a telephone at home. It was a wooden box with a (　　　　) on its side.
2. I found that a person named "Information Please" lived in the telephone (　　　　) and that she knew everything.
3. I was playing with a (　　　　), and then I hit my finger. The (　　　　) was terrible, but nobody was home but me.

Part 2 　教科書 p.176〜p.177 　　/54

A　Write the English words to match the Japanese.　【知識・技能（語彙）】（各2点）

1. .... 動 返事をする B1　　2. .... 名 地理 B1
3. .... 動 …をなだめる B1　　4. .... 名 塊 B2
5. .... 名 羽, 羽毛 A2　　6. .... 副 どういうわけか, なぜか B1

B　Choose the word whose stressed syllable is different from the other three.

【知識・技能（発音）】（各2点）

1. ア . con-cern　　　　　イ . cor-rect　　　ウ . ex-plore　　　エ . for-tune
2. ア . ca-nar-y　　　　　イ . per-son-al　　　ウ . pri-ma-ry　　　エ . ter-ri-ble
3. ア . en-ter-tain-ment　イ . ge-og-ra-phy　ウ . in-flu-en-tial　エ . sit-u-a-tion

C　Complete the following English sentences to match the Japanese.

【知識・技能（表現・文法）】（完答・各3点）

1. 今や子供たちはもう家を出て行ったので，私たちはもっと小さな家に引っ越すことができます。

   (　　　　) (　　　　　) the children have left home, we can move to a smaller house.
2. 彼は東京で生まれたが，北海道で育った。

   He was born in Tokyo, but (　　　　　) (　　　　　) in Hokkaido.
3. 兄は高校生の頃とても人気があったにちがいない。

   My brother (　　　　　) (　　　　　) (　　　　　　) very popular when he was a high school student.

D　Arrange the words in the proper order to match the Japanese. 【知識・技能（表現・文法）】（各4点）

1. チョコレートをもう一かけら割り取ってくれませんか。

   Could you (another / bit / break / chocolate / of / off) for me?

   ----

2. それらのかばんを運ぶのを手伝いましょうか。

   Do you (help / me / those / to / want / with / you) bags?

   ----

3. 彼はチケット売り場に早く着いたが，残念なことに，ショーのチケットはすでに売り切れだと言われた。

   He arrived early at the ticket office only (all / be / that / the tickets / to / told) for the show had already been sold out.

E　Fill in each blank with a suitable word from the passage.【思考力・判断力・表現力（内容）】（各5点）

1. I called Information Please and told her what had happened to me.　She was (　　　　) enough to tell me what to do.
2. After my first experience with Information Please, I asked her for some help when I had some questions in (　　　　) or arithmetic.
3. When our pet (　　　　) died, I felt sad.　I told her the sad story, and she tried to (　　　　) me.

Part 3　教科書 p.178〜p.179　　/54

A　Write the English words to match the Japanese.　【知識・技能（語彙）】（各2点）

1. ....　形 聞き慣れた, 馴染みの A2　　2. ....　名 瞬間
3. ....　動 …をびっくりさせる, 驚かせる B1　4. ....　動 …を怖がらせる A2
5. ....　名 ポンポン，なでなで　　6. ....　形 細長い，細い

B　Choose the word whose underlined part's sound is different from the other three.

【知識・技能（発音）】（各2点）

1. ア．c<u>a</u>ncer　　　　イ．ch<u>a</u>nce　　　　ウ．h<u>a</u>mmer　　　　エ．l<u>a</u>ter
2. ア．<u>o</u>perator　　　イ．pr<u>o</u>blem　　　　ウ．tr<u>ou</u>ble　　　　エ．v<u>o</u>lume
3. ア．qu<u>ar</u>ter　　　イ．sc<u>a</u>re　　　　ウ．sc<u>o</u>re　　　　エ．w<u>ar</u>n

C　Complete the following English sentences to match the Japanese.

【知識・技能（表現・文法）】（完答・各3点）

1. 彼ははしごから芝生の上へ落ちた。

He (　　　　) (　　　　) the ladder onto the grass.

2. 私たちはかつては仲のよい友達でしたが，もはや友達ではありません。

We used to be good friends, but we are (　　　　) (　　　　) friends.

3. 私は政治にはまったく興味がありません。

I am not (　　　　) (　　　　) interested in politics.

D　Arrange the words in the proper order to match the Japanese.　【知識・技能（表現・文法）】（各4点）

1. 2人の人が議論するとき，それぞれは相手が間違っていると確信している。

When two people argue, each (is / is / sure / that / the other person) wrong.

---

2. その火事を消すのに数時間かかった。

It took several hours (bring / control / the fire / to / under).

---

3. その子はイヌの頭を軽くたたいた。

The child (a pat / gave / on / the dog / the head).

E　Fill in each blank with a suitable word from the passage.　【思考力・判断力・表現力（内容）】（各5点）

1. Another day I asked Information Please how to (　　　　) "fix."
2. At that moment, my sister jumped off the (　　　　) at me. I fell down and pulled the (　　　） out of the box.
3. Minutes later, a telephone (　　　　) came. I told him what happened and he did his repair work.

Part 4　教科書 p.180〜p.181　　/54

A　Write the English words to match the Japanese.　【知識・技能（語彙）】（各2点）

1. ....　图 疑問 A2
2. ....　動 …を思い出す B1
3. ....　形 落ち着いた，平和な B2
4. ....　動 …をありがたく思う，…を感謝する A2
5. ....　副 不思議にも，奇跡的にも
6. ....　形 ばかばかしい，ばかげた A2

B　Choose the word whose stressed syllable is different from the other three.

【知識・技能（発音）】（各2点）

1. ア．be-long　　イ．mo-ment　　ウ．re-spect　　エ．se-rene
2. ア．fi-nal-ly　　イ．mem-o-ry　　ウ．Pa-cif-ic　　エ．ter-ri-fy
3. ア．ap-pre-ci-ate　イ．cer-e-mo-ny　ウ．i-den-ti-ty　エ．se-cur-i-ty

C　Complete the following English sentences to match the Japanese.

【知識・技能（表現・文法）】（完答・各3点）

1. 私が最後にその村を訪れてから多くの変化が起こっている。

A lot of changes have (　　　　) (　　　　) since I last visited the village.

2. ジョージは転職しようかと考えている。

George is (　　　　) (　　　　) changing jobs.

3. 若い頃，彼はよくここらの林を散歩したものだ。

When he was young, he (　　　　) (　　　　) walk in these woods.

D　Arrange the words in the proper order to match the Japanese.　【知識・技能（表現・文法）】（各4点）

1. 彼女がだれにもさよならも言わずに帰って行ったのには驚いた。

I was surprised that she left (anyone / goodbye / saying / to / without).

2. 隣の部屋から怒った声が聞こえてきた。

We (an angry voice / coming / from / heard / the next room).

3. こんなことにこれ以上時間をむだ使いするのはよしましょう。

Let's not (any / more time / on / this / waste).

E　Fill in each blank with a suitable word from the passage.【思考力・判断力・表現力（内容）】（各5点）

1. I grew into my (　　　　), and yet I couldn't forget my good childhood (　　　　) with Information Please.

2. A few years later, I was on my way to college in the west. I called my hometown (　　　　) and heard that small, clear voice, saying, "(　　　　)."

3. It was the same woman. We talked about how much we (　　　　) (　　　　) each other.

Part 5 　教科書 p.182〜p.183　　/44

A Write the English words to match the Japanese. 【知識・技能（語彙）】（各2点）

1. .... 图 学期 A2

B Choose the word whose stressed syllable is different from the other three.

【知識・技能（発音）】（各2点）

1. ア. ef-fect 　　イ. mes-sage 　　ウ. pre-vent 　　エ. sup-port
2. ア. ad-vance 　　イ. ef-fort 　　ウ. in-sect 　　エ. mod-ern
3. ア. con-sump-tion 　イ. dif-fer-ent 　ウ. se-mes-ter 　エ. to-geth-er

C Complete the following English sentences to match the Japanese.

【知識・技能（表現・文法）】（完答・各3点）

1. この番号に電話して，サリーをお願いしますと言ってね。

   Phone this number and (　　　　) (　　　　) Sally.
2. 彼に伝言を残しますか。

   Would you like to (　　　) a (　　　　) for him?
3. 旅行の計画はいつも前もって立てておくべきです。

   You should always plan your trips (　　　) (　　　　).

D Arrange the words in the proper order to match the Japanese. 【知識・技能（表現・文法）】（各4点）

1. 残念ですが，あなたの申し込みはお断りさせていただきます。

   I'm (sorry / tell / that / to / you) your application has been unsuccessful.

   ----

2. 私が何も言えないうちに，スティーヴは歩き去って行きました。

   (anything / before / could / I / say), Steve walked away.

   ----

3. きみと偶然会えてよかった。明日の歴史の試験についてきみに聞きたいことがあったんだ。

   (am / glad / I / I / into / ran / you). I wanted to ask you about tomorrow's history test.

E Fill in each blank with a suitable word from the passage.

【思考力・判断力・表現力（内容）】（完答・各5点）

1. Three months passed, and I was back at the Seattle airport. When I called Information Please, I heard a (　　　　) voice.
2. The woman told me that Sally had been (　　　　) and had passed away five weeks before.
3. She also read out the (　　　　) Sally had left for me. It said, "There are other worlds to (　　　) in." I understood what Sally meant.

84

総合問題

/30

Read the following passage and answer the questions below.

All this took place in a small town in the Pacific Northwest. Then, when I was nine years old, we moved across the country to Boston —— and I missed Information Please very much. She belonged in that old wooden box back home, and I somehow never thought of trying the tall, skinny new phone that sat on a small table in the hall.

(　1　), as I grew into my teens, the memories of those childhood conversations never really left me; often in moments of doubt and worry I would recall the serene sense of security I had when I knew that I could call Information Please and get the right answer. I appreciated now how patient, understanding and kind she was to have wasted her time (　A　) a little boy.

A few years later, on my way west to college, my plane landed in Seattle. I had about half an hour before my plane left, and I (B)(15 minutes / on / or / so / spent / the phone) with my sister, who had a happy marriage there now. (　2　), really without thinking what I was doing, I dialed my hometown operator and said, "Information Please."

(　3　), I heard again the small, clear voice I knew so well: "Information."

I hadn't planned this, but I heard myself saying, "Could you tell me, please, how to spell the word 'fix'?"

There was a long pause. Then came the softly spoken answer. "I guess," said Information Please, "that your finger must be all right (　C　) now."

I laughed. "(　4　) it's really still you. I wonder if you have any idea how much you meant (　D　) me during all that time …"

"I wonder," she replied, "if you know how much you meant (　D　) me? I never had any children, and I used to look forward to your calls. Silly, wasn't it?"

---

1. 空所(1), (2), (3), (4)に入る適切な語を語群から選んで答えなさい。　【知識・技能（文法）】（各2点）

   (1) (　　　　　　　　)　　(2) (　　　　　　　　)　　(3) (　　　　　　　　)　　(4) (　　　　　　　　)

   〔 Miraculously,　So,　Then,　Yet 〕

2. 空所(A), (C), (D)に入る適切な語を選びなさい。　【知識・技能（文法）】（各2点）

   (A)　ア．at　　　　イ．for　　　　ウ．on　　　　エ．to

   (C)　ア．at　　　　イ．by　　　　ウ．for　　　　エ．on

   (D)　ア．for　　　　イ．in　　　　ウ．to　　　　エ．with

3. 下線部(B)の（　　）内の語句を適切に並べかえなさい。　【知識・技能（文法）】（6点）

---

4. 本文の内容と合っていないものをすべて選びなさい。　【思考力・判断力・表現力（内容）】（完答・10点）

   ア．The author felt sorry that he had made Information Please waste her time.

   イ．The author often remembered the sense of security that Information Please had given to him.

   ウ．Information Please and the author meant a lot to each other.

   エ．Information Please was tired of waiting for the author's calls.